T0312323

Cambridge Elements ☰

Elements in Metaphysics
edited by
Tuomas E. Tahko
University of Bristol

MODALITY

Sònia Roca-Royes
University of Stirling

CAMBRIDGE
UNIVERSITY PRESS

CAMBRIDGE
UNIVERSITY PRESS

Shaftesbury Road, Cambridge CB2 8EA, United Kingdom

One Liberty Plaza, 20th Floor, New York, NY 10006, USA

477 Williamstown Road, Port Melbourne, VIC 3207, Australia

314–321, 3rd Floor, Plot 3, Splendor Forum, Jasola District Centre,
New Delhi – 110025, India

103 Penang Road, #05–06/07, Visioncrest Commercial, Singapore 238467

Cambridge University Press is part of Cambridge University Press & Assessment,
a department of the University of Cambridge.

We share the University's mission to contribute to society through the pursuit of
education, learning and research at the highest international levels of excellence.

www.cambridge.org
Information on this title: www.cambridge.org/9781009001304

DOI: 10.1017/9781009004596

First published 2023

A catalogue record for this publication is available from the British Library.

ISBN 978-1-009-00130-4 Paperback
ISSN 2633-9862 (online)
ISSN 2633-9854 (print)

Cambridge University Press & Assessment has no responsibility for the persistence
or accuracy of URLs for external or third-party internet websites referred to in this
publication and does not guarantee that any content on such websites is, or will
remain, accurate or appropriate.

Modality

Elements in Metaphysics

DOI: 10.1017/9781009004596
First published online: April 2023

Sònia Roca-Royes
University of Stirling
Author for correspondence: Sònia Roca-Royes, sonia.rocaroyes@stir.ac.uk

Abstract: Modality is a vast phenomenon. In fact, it is arguably a plurality of phenomena. Within it, one type of modality warrants distinctive interest in philosophy and, in particular, in metaphysics. In view of this, Section 2 of this Element is devoted to modality as a general phenomenon; different types of modalities are distinguished, and the question of unification is raised. Following this, Section 3 is focused on metaphysical modality: the type of modality that is of distinctive interest in metaphysics, and thus for this Elements series. In Section 3, the overarching question is about the source of metaphysical modality, and the discussion here informs, and is informed by, the question of unification discussed in Section 2. This title is also available as open access on Cambridge Core.

Keywords: modality, essence, alethic modalities, epistemic modalities, metaphysical modality, deontic modalities, possible worlds, disposition, de dicto/de re

ISBNs: 9781009001304 (PB), 9781009004596 (OC)
ISSNs: 2633-9862 (online), 2633-9854 (print)

Contents

1 Introduction

Have you ever wondered why you use a safety belt when travelling by car? Or why a child decides against stealing something they desperately want yet their parents wouldn't buy? Modal cognition is typically at the core of such decisions. We know that any of us *could* have a car accident and that a properly worn safety belt decreases human harm in case there is one. This knowledge informs our decision to use the safety belt. (Or, for otherwise inclined subjects, the *possibility* of a fine would play a similar role.) Analogously, the child knows they *might* be caught, and the fear of punishment if they are caught has the power to bend their immature moral will. We usually *take it for granted* that these decisions are rational, and our doing so is partly explained by our belief that those possibilities *are* so and that modal cognisers are, by and large, justified in their modal beliefs.

But *what is modality* in the first place? This is the question at the core of the present Element, and I shall approach it in a two-tier manner, with cumulative effect: first, I focus on modality in general and, after that, on metaphysical modality in particular – arguably the kind of modality which is distinctively central to metaphysics.

Crudely put, modality refers to modes; modes, for instance, in which a proposition can be true or a property possessed: necessarily or contingently. More generally, modality in philosophy is the area that studies the notions of *necessity, possibility*, and *contingency* (plus cognates). But modality is a vast phenomenon and, within it, we can distinguish different types, even families, such as deontic, epistemic, and alethic. And depending on which of these families is our focus on a given occasion, our modal investigations will also lead us into studying related notions such as *essence, accident, disposition, power, permission, obligation, norm, knowledge*, and *evidence*, among others.

Which family of modalities is most central in a given philosophical context depends on the branch of philosophy under consideration: deontic modalities, for instance, are likely to be more central to ethics than to general epistemology. In metaphysics – the series in which this Element is situated – alethic modalities are largely central and, among them, *metaphysical* modality is distinctively so. But modality as a *general* phenomenon already raises very interesting questions, including metaphysical ones, that wouldn't vividly manifest if one were to focus on alethic or, within it, metaphysical modality from the outset. Section 2 of this Element is thus devoted to the general phenomenon. In it, we will look into questions such as what it is that brings all different kinds of modality together: what is it, if anything, that makes all kinds of modality, kinds of *modality*? Is there a fundamental modality among them? The contemporary literature is interestingly divided about this and, by way of anticipation, we will see that positions on the matter are not independent of one's stance on the source of metaphysical modality. This section will thus inform Section 3, which focuses, more narrowly, on different views on the source of *metaphysical* modality. Section 3 will also evidence (albeit only in passing) how questions about the metaphysics of modality can be impacted by epistemological concerns; i.e., concerns about our knowledge of modality.

2 Modalities

2.1 Variety of Modal Discourses

Modal discourse is ubiquitous and it is very much entrenched in our daily lives. We have considered a couple of examples in the Introduction, and it is not difficult to come up with a much longer list of scenarios where modal propositions (or modal beliefs) are at the core of our reasoning or decision-making processes. As crudely characterised in the Introduction, a modal proposition involves some modal notion – central among them are *possibility* and *necessity*. In the following, it is the absence of modal notions in (1) and their presence in (2) that makes only the second proposition a modal one:[1]

(1) Iris' knee is bleeding.

(2) The fall *must* have been worse than it looked.

As with any other type of proposition, modal propositions can be true or false. Regardless of their truth-value, all the propositions below are modal in virtue of each involving a modal notion:

(3) Iris *could* be more careful.

(4) Two plus five *must* be seven.

(5) One *can't* always be a Good Samaritan.

(6) Being a philosopher is *accidental* to Socrates.

(7) A rocket *can* travel faster than light.

(8) *Necessarily*, if Ernest isn't married, he is a bachelor.

(9) You *can* drive without a safety belt when you're heavily pregnant.

(10) If Ernest isn't married, he's *necessarily* a bachelor.

(11) Umar *can't* be at the hospital.

(12) You *can* jump this stream.

(13) You *must* respect people's turns (e.g., in a queue).

(14) It *must* have been raining.

(15) You *can't* torture people.

---

[1] It will do no harm here not to distinguish between propositions and sentences expressing them.

These propositions, and some contrasts among them, will first serve us to illustrate the ubiquity of modal discourse, and they will then help us draw distinctions between different types of modalities (Sections 2.2, 2.3, and 2.4). Following this, we will tackle the much-contested issue of *unification* (Sections 2.5 and 2.6) and use this discussion to reflect on the contemporary role of *possible worlds* (Section 2.7) and the prospects of precisifying, within modality, the *de re*/*de dicto* distinction (Section 2.8).

Of the propositions above, some might seem artificial (they have been chosen with a purpose) but others are ordinary modal propositions and it's not difficult to conceive of scenarios where one might easily apply them. For example, someone tells you that your neighbour, Umar, was admitted into hospital yesterday night with severe Covid-19; this surprises you as you've just spoken to him on the phone this morning. You reply with (11) – Umar *can't* be at the hospital. In a second example, your daughter is playing in the park, which is divided by a stream. She's on one side, but wants to join a group of children who are playing on the other side. She's impatient, and wonders whether to walk down to the bridge, cross it, and walk up again, or whether she should dare jumping across the stream. After assessing the circumstances, you encourage her with (12) – You *can* jump this stream. And a third example: your nephew enters a busy candy shop and goes straight to the counter demanding a lollipop. You intervene with (13) – You *must* respect people's turns.

These are just a couple of examples. They may be trivial, but they are illustrative of how quotidian modal thought and modal reasoning is. Beyond quotidian life, preventive medicine is a health specialisation whose goal is to prevent people from contracting illnesses they *can* (relatively easily) contract. At a more abstract level, modal reasoning is central in scientific methodology. The process of acquiring information about how the world *is* can be seen as the process of ruling out that the world is some other *possible* way. Let us suppose that there are two hypotheses, H_1 and H_2, that seem to equally explain our body of evidence, E. For all we know, the world could be like H_1 says, but it also could be like H_2 says. If we want to know how the world is, and given that evidence E is neutral between H_1 and H_2, we need disambiguating evidence. This extra evidence can be achieved by designing and carrying out experiments; this is common scientific practice. And yet, designing and carrying out experiments can be very costly (financially and otherwise). Could we justify this practice if we had sufficient reasons to believe that either H_1 or H_2 are impossible? Or if we had sufficient reasons to rule one out? When a hypothesis is taken seriously, we are assuming, at least implicitly, that the world *could* be the way the hypothesis describes it.

The reader who is already familiar with the distinction between *alethic*, *epistemic*, and *deontic* modalities might be wondering why I'm not being more rigorous. Is it epistemic or alethic possibilities that are being assumed in scientific practice, for instance? Is it in an epistemic sense or in a physical sense that Umar can't be at the hospital? However, this lack of rigour, at this stage, is intended. It illustrates that there are indeed different senses associated with our modal vocabulary, and which one is involved easily varies from context to context (including a speaker's intentions). Consider again proposition (11) – Umar *can't* be at the hospital. Is this true or false? This question cannot be answered once and for all; it depends on the sense (and context) in which it is uttered. For instance, above, I pictured a context intended to be one where an utterance of (11) is very likely to be true. *If you know* that you've heard Umar at home this morning, talking on the phone, then (it is likely that) *he couldn't* have been admitted into hospital with severe Covid-19 the evening prior. There *must* have been a misunderstanding somewhere: maybe he was checked but not kept in? The sense of modality in which these conclusions are true is, as we shall see shortly, an epistemic one: it is dependent on what we know.

But (11) could be uttered in other contexts where we don't mean an epistemic sense of 'can'. Imagine a group of friends and one of them, Shyla, asks where Umar is. Joel replies: 'Well, he's quite healthy, so he can't be in the hospital', to which Kiran protests that his being quite healthy doesn't mean that he cannot fall ill or have an accident. In this context, (11), as uttered by Joel, is likely to be false, and what makes it false is not dependent on what the group of friends *know* or *believe about* Umar, but rather on what's modally *true of* him: regardless of his degree of health, Umar, as an organism, is not immune to illnesses or accidents. As we will also see shortly, this dependence on *truth* makes this sense of modality an alethic one. In addition to the epistemic and the alethic, there's yet another kind of modality that we will also focus on in this section: the deontic one, which has to do with *norms*. To get a taste of it, consider (15) – You *can't* torture people. If this strikes you as true, you're most likely reading it in the deontic sense, and, if so, the message you're taking from it is that it's not morally permissible to torture people. Notice that, in an alethic sense, (15) is false: as too often witnessed, there aren't many physical impediments to people torturing others.

It is the aim of the next three sections (Sections 2.2, 2.3, and 2.4) to unfold these brief remarks by focusing on three main families of modalities: epistemic, deontic, and alethic. I shall first introduce them separately. After this, in Sections 2.5 and 2.6, I will be most interested in exploring the relations between them, paying special attention to debates in recent literature having to do with the prospects of finding a unifying treatment. Before all this, let me introduce the notions of *possibility* and *necessity* as duals of one another. Roughly, by 'duality' in this context we mean that we can define *possibility* in terms of *necessity*, and vice versa.[2] Specifically, *p is possible* – in symbols, ◊p – means that it is not necessary that not p – in symbols, ¬□¬p. We have just defined possibility in terms of necessity. And we can correspondingly define necessity in terms of possibility: *p is necessary* (□p) means that it is not possible that not p (¬◊¬p). With duality in place, let us turn to the different types of modalities.

2.2 Epistemic Modalities

Assuming the duality between *possibility* and *necessity*, it is open to us to directly characterise the *epistemic* sense of only one of the two modal notions – necessity or possibility – and to arrive at the other by means of the conceptual path that their duality affords. I shall illustrate this as we move along, starting with the notion of epistemic *possibility*. As a first approximation, epistemic possibility can be characterised in the following way:

Epistemic possibility (EP):
A proposition, *p*, is epistemically possible for a subject, S, if and only if *p* is (logically) compatible with all S knows.

It is this dependence on *knowledge* that gives epistemic modality its name, from the ancient Greek *episteme*, meaning knowledge or science. The first thing to note is that (EP) characterises *epistemic possibility* as relative to a subject. This cannot be otherwise due, precisely, to its dependence on a given subject's body of knowledge. Note also that, since different subjects will clearly know different things, which propositions are (or are not) epistemically possible will vary accordingly across subjects. To illustrate: if I have no idea what is the highest speed a spur-thighed tortoise can reach, it's epistemically possible *for me* that Clark (my friend's spur-thighed tortoise) walked at three kilometres per hour yesterday; such speed is certainly compatible with all I know – virtually nothing – about tortoises. However, a herpetologist will have relevant information about tortoises that puts her in a position to rule out that Clark ever reached that speed. Thus, it is *not* epistemically possible *for the herpetologist* that Clark walked at three kilometres per hour yesterday.

(EP) is a good first approximation. It captures a kind of epistemic modality often made salient in ordinary contexts, as the Umar example above and the tortoise case just described, serve to illustrate. Given that we're assuming the duality of the notions of necessity and possibility, we now have two options to characterise the corresponding *epistemic necessity*: we either characterise it

---

[2] This is widely but not universally accepted. Arthur Prior, for instance, developed a modal logic where □p is not even *extensionally* equivalent to ¬◊¬p. (See system Q in Prior 1957.)

directly, or else we do it from (EP), exploiting the duality. The two ways will (and should, if the duality is such) be extensionally equivalent:

Epistemic Necessity (EN), directly:
A proposition, p, is epistemically necessary for S if and only if p (logically) follows from what S knows.

Epistemic Necessity (EN), exploiting the duality:
A proposition, p, is epistemically necessary for S if and only if it is not epistemically possible for S that not p.

(EP) and (EN) jointly characterise what is perhaps the most paradigmatic type of epistemic modality. To be rigorous, however, they characterise potentially as many different epistemic modalities as there are individuals (or, more rigorously, as there are pairs of individuals and times). For what we've got is a *schema*, rather than a modality, and we can replace 'S' by any individual, each of these moves resulting in an epistemic modality.

But even leaving this schematicity to one side, this schema (of epistemic modalities relativised to one single individual) is not the only one within the family of epistemic modalities, not even the one that will always be salient. Sometimes, the context might make salient instead an epistemic modality relativised to a *group* of individuals. To capture these other types of epistemic modalities, we would need to mention explicitly a group of individuals in the schema. In addition, we would need to accompany this by an unambiguous notion of collective knowledge. This gives rise to alternative, non-equivalent (schemas of) epistemic modalities, as the following illustrates without being exhaustive:

*Epistemic Possibility, relativised to groups, **intersection**:*
A proposition, p, is epistemically possible for a group of people G if and only if p is (logically) compatible with what every member in G knows.

*Epistemic Possibility, relativised to groups, **union**:*
A proposition, p, is epistemically possible for a group of people G if and only if p is (logically) compatible with what *some* member in G knows.

As above, these are schemas. In order to get an epistemic modality from them, we would need to plug in a given group of people in each case. Technically, for any group of people we can think of, we could plug it in, and we would obtain a specific epistemic modality as a result. Admittedly, some of these modalities are of greater interest than others. For instance, in the middle of a pandemic, plugging in a worldwide group of epidemiologists would generate a much more interesting epistemic modality (in either the union or the intersection sense) than the group of members in my household, especially with respect to possibilities concerning, for instance, how stressed hospitals will be in a year's time, or how risky it is to book a flight for two months' time.

We have focused so far on epistemic modalities in a strict sense: that is, modalities that are dependent on *knowledge*. One might wonder what the result would be if we considered alternative notions in the vicinity, such as *belief*, or even *justified belief*. The answer, simply put, is that we would get different types of modalities which, with a suitably relaxed understanding of the label 'epistemic modality', might still be taken to be such, and for which, with a more stringent insistence on labels, 'doxastic modalities' would be more apt. Regardless of our terminological choices, all these modalities have in common their relativisation to an individual or group of individuals, and that what is possible or necessary for them depends on the *body of information* that the individuals are committed to, at least at the level of belief. This makes all the elements in this (relaxed) group of modalities quite close to one another as phenomena.

And yet, one interesting difference between epistemic modalities and doxastic ones (in stringent senses of these labels), stems from the facticity of knowledge and the lack of facticity of belief (even of justified belief). We know that what is known is indeed the case – knowledge is factive – but that beliefs, even justified ones, can be false – belief is not factive. This difference has a sharp impact on the *modal logics* that can be used to model epistemic and doxastic modalities. Think of the principle according to which *what's necessary is (also) the case*, which is known as principle (M) in modal logic (in symbols, $\Box p \rightarrow p$). With a *stringent-epistemic* sense of 'necessary' this principle comes out as *valid* (cannot fail to be true), but this is not the case with the *doxastic* sense of the term. We will take the cases in turn. If p is *epistemically* necessary (if $\Box p$, in the epistemic sense), then p follows from a body of knowledge (be that knowledge of a single individual or of a group of individuals). Since knowledge is factive, p is the case. As a result, if $\Box p$ then p. And since the choice of p was arbitrary, this concludes the reasoning for the epistemic sense. By contrast, if p is *doxastically* necessary (if $\Box p$, in the doxastic sense), then certainly p follows from a body of beliefs, but this is insufficient to guarantee the truth of p; indeed, p could be falsely believed (that is, the body of information from where p follows could be false). As a result, in the doxastic case, we cannot safely transition from $\Box p$ to p: some of these transitions could lead us from truth to falsehood. Things being so, if one is to model *epistemic* modality with modal logic, it will need to be with a modal logic that includes principle (M), whereas one would need to exclude it if one is modelling *doxastic* modalities.[3] We will return to (M) when considering deontic modalities, to which we now turn.

---

[3] It is important to distinguish the *validity* of a principle from its *truth*. Beliefs can be falsely held, but they can also be truly held. Does this mean that the principle is valid in a world where (M)

2.3 Deontic Modalities

Deontic modalities, you will recall from Section 2.1, have to do with permission and obligation. Recall proposition (15): You *can't* torture people.

In a physical sense of 'can', one certainly can torture people. The sense in which (15) is intended to be true is rather a deontic one: it's not *permitted* for you to torture people (or, exploiting the duality from Section 2.1, it is an *obligation* for you not to do so). As with epistemic modalities, and as the plural indicates, deontic modalities constitute a family, unified by the fact that they all relate to permission and obligation. Any code of conduct – in a school, at work, at home, in relation to a game, in a state, in a community, etc. – amounts to a deontic modality. Among the many members in this family, *moral* modality and *legal* modality are most salient. In the moral sense, (15) tells us that torturing people would amount to transgressing a moral principle. In the legal sense, (15) tells us that torturing people is not allowed by a given system of (man-made) laws. Even these types of modalities are, yet again, families: there's not just one system of (man-made) laws in the world, but many; each state (and not only states) has its own set. And, regardless of whether or not there is an absolute (universal) moral code, in an equally legitimate use of the term 'morality', there are various moralities; these are quite often associated with (but not limited to) the variety of religions.

A schema for deontic possibilities can thus be as follows:

p is C-possible if and only if *p* is (logically) compatible with all the elements in C (where C encodes a given code of conduct).

This schema allows us to see a structural difference compared with epistemic modalities: deontic modalities are not relativised to individuals in the way epistemic modalities are.

To give a couple of examples, consider *Christian morality*, according to which you shall not murder, you shall not steal, you shall not commit adultery, etc. We can call 'ChM' the code of conduct encoded in the Ten Commandments. Similar to what we did with epistemic modalities, we can now characterise Christian-Morality modality as follows:

p is Christian-morally possible if and only if it is (logically) compatible with all the elements in ChM.
p is Christian-morally necessary if and only if it (logically) follows from the elements in ChM.

---

doesn't have false instances? The answer is 'no'. It will always be *possible* for it to have false instances, and this possibility *invalidates* the principle qua principle.

It follows from the above characterisation that it is Christian-morally necessary that Cain doesn't kill Abel. And yet (assuming for the sake of the example that what we have heard about them is true), Cain killed Abel. We can thus identify a proposition – Cain doesn't kill Abel – that is both necessary, in the current sense of the term, and fails to be true. As such, this proposition alone suffices to compromise the validity of principle (M), □p→p, for the current modality; and it doesn't take much imagination to identify a whole battery of other propositions with the same effect.

Scottish-Legal modality, to give one further example, behaves similarly. Let us call the Scottish Legal system 'SLS'. We can then characterise Scottish-Legal possibility as that which is compatible with all the elements in SLS. According to SLS, drink-driving is an offence and, as such, the proposition *that Finley drove home while noticeably drunk* is Scottish-Legally impossible. Despite such status, in a physical sense of 'possible', it's certainly possible for him – and anyone – to drive home while noticeably drunk. Any instance of drink-driving in Scotland is proof of the invalidity of principle (M) for the case of Scottish-Legal modality.

These reasonings generalise to any deontic modality. Indeed, *deontic modalities* all have in common with *doxastic modalities* their invalidation of principle (M): just as there's no guarantee that people (will) believe truly, there's also no guarantee that people (will) do what they deontically must. It is characteristic of deontic modalities that their *musts* can typically (in a physical sense) be transgressed. As we will see in the next section, this feature distinguishes *alethic modalities* from *deontic modalities*.

2.4 Alethic Modalities

In comparison to epistemic modalities, which, as seen in Section 2.2, can be characterised as dependent upon a given body of knowledge (or beliefs), alethic modalities can be characterised instead as dependent on a body of *truths*. And it is this feature which gives alethic modalities their name – from the ancient Greek *aletheia*, for truth. The schema for them is very similar to that in the case of deontic modalities and, in particular, they share with the deontic family that they are not relativised to individuals:

p is C-possible if and only if it is (logically) compatible with all the elements in C (where C is a given set of *truths*).

There are several questions that soon appear when trying to structurally characterise alethic modalities. An important issue, which will shape our discussion here and be relevant in much of Section 2.5, can be informed by the following remarks.

Consider the epistemic modalities in the stricter sense; those dependent on *knowledge*. As will be appreciated, potentially any set of true propositions, so long as they are graspable, can constitute a body of information known by some individual (or group). As a consequence, the family of epistemic modalities is potentially vast. And even if it might not *actually* be as vast, it is no doubt already very large: there are many people in the world, and any variation – no matter how slight – in the body of knowledge of any two people will determine different epistemic modalities. The question is: can we say something similar about the family of *alethic modalities*? That is, is there an alethic modality for any (whichever) set of truths? This question is important. It is also a controversial issue that cannot be answered in a theoretically neutral way. For this reason, I shall postpone addressing it until Section 2.5, when we will look into the question whether there is something that *unifies* the different types of modalities (different answers to this question have different implications about the size of the family of alethic modalities). For the time being, I shall focus on some *typical* (and some less typical) examples of alethic modalities. These examples raise their own controversies, some of which are deserving of more attention than they have been given so far. (As a note of caution, please bear in mind that, as in Sections 2.2 and 2.3, I'll be talking about ways of *characterising* (alethic) modalities, not ways of *defining* them. More on this in Section 2.5.)

2.4.1 Nomic Modality

The term 'nomic modality' comes from the Greek *nomos*, meaning law. One could make the point that there are various types of laws (recall for instance our use of the term 'law' in Section 2.3, within the context of deontic modalities) and that, as a result, 'nomic modality' could potentially refer to several *families* of modalities. While this is so, it is also true that, in the context of modalities, 'nomic modality' is usually taken to refer to one particular type of alethic modality: the one related to the *laws of nature*. This is partly stipulative, and I shall simply follow standard practice. Given nomic modality's relation to the laws of nature, it is often referred to as 'physical modality' and also 'natural modality', and I will use these three labels interchangeably. With this remark in place, let LN be the set of natural laws (or an axiomatisation of them). In a way that is structurally similar to what we have done above, we can characterise nomic possibility and nomic necessity, directly, as follows. For any p,

p is nomically necessary if and only if it (logically) follows from the elements in LN.
p is nomically possible if and only if it is (logically) compatible with all the elements in LN.

Presumably, one of the elements in LN says that no object travels at a speed faster than that of light. Consider now the proposition that *there is a meteor approaching Earth at a speed twice that of light*. This proposition is incompatible with LN and, as a result, it will be regarded as nomically impossible. However, here is a somewhat tricky example that will call for a slight refinement of the characterisation above: *Meteor 211 does not approach Earth at a speed twice that of light*. This example is tricky because the elements in LN are presumably all generalisations with little or no mention of specific individuals. In particular, Meteor 211 is not mentioned. As a result, strictly speaking, the proposition that *Meteor 211 does not approach Earth at a speed twice that of light* doesn't follow from LN. And yet, considering it to be nomically contingent would be widely taken to be an inadequate result. The laws might not mention particular individuals, but they nonetheless affect them all (the existent ones at any rate). To manage this and other similar cases, we should therefore understand (hence the refinement) that a proposition *p* is nomically necessary iff *p* follows from the elements in LN plus *the existence* of the individuals mentioned in *p* (if any). From a logical perspective, this would amount to having an axiom stating the existence of Meteor 211: there is something, x, that Meteor 211 is identical to.

So far so good. But here is a more controversial example which I shall present neutrally (because of the controversy it generates), and that will give us material for Section 2.5, where we explore the potential unification of several alethic modalities. What about the proposition that *Socrates is a dog*? Is this compatible with the elements in LN? Again, given that the laws of nature are generalisations with no mention of particular individuals, the answer appears to be 'yes': Socrates being a dog doesn't contradict them. The reason why this example is trickier than the previous one (and cannot be similarly accommodated) is two-fold.

First, many modal metaphysicians would be inclined to think of this proposition as nomically impossible. The reason for this would be akin to the following: it would be assumed that (i) nomic possibility implies metaphysical possibility, but believed that (ii) *Socrates is a dog* is metaphysically impossible and, consequently, that (iii) it is also nomically impossible.

Second, however, is the fact just mentioned that the elements in LN are generalisations with little or no mention of specific individuals. There might be biological laws to the effect that dogs bark, that humans are mammals (perhaps even that humans are not dogs), etc. But such laws are not incompatible with the proposition that *Socrates is a dog* – not even when taking into account Socrates' existence (i.e., not even when adding the axiom that there is something, x, that Socrates is identical to).[4] So the proposition comes out as nomically possible.

Thus, as anticipated, this example resists being treated on a par with how we treated the example about Meteor 211. The controversy is now whether or not to count *Socrates is a dog* as nomically impossible, and each option seems to impose some revision: either on the characterisation of the notion, or else on its extension. For the standard conception of nomic modality is the thin one above: crudely, that nomic possibility is a matter of compatibility with the laws of nature. But since this thin conception is not enough to sanction *Socrates is a dog* as nomically *im*possible, a thicker notion of nomic possibility is needed. Or else, one would need to embrace the *nomic* possibility of Socrates being a dog.

To clarify: the difference between this example and the previous one boils down to the different logical forms of the laws that are (or *would be*) involved in generating the impossibility. In the meteor example, the relevant law is the generalisation of an unconditional statement (i.e., $\forall x \neg Px$, where P stands for the property of travelling faster than a certain speed). By contrast, in the Socrates case, the laws that could potentially generate the impossibility are generalisations of a *conditional* statement (e.g., $\forall x(Hx \rightarrow \neg Dx)$, where H and D stand for *human* and *dog* respectively). And this difference accounts for the fact that, in the Socrates case, a mere axiom stating the existence of Socrates does not imply his satisfaction of the antecedent, H. What *would* generate the nomic impossibility of Socrates being a dog would be (in combination with LN) the proposition that *Socrates is human* (provided, as we are granting, that LN includes a law to the effect that humans are not dogs). But to introduce the proposition that Socrates is human in characterising the notion of nomic modality would be contrary to the thin understanding of the notion: as having to do with the laws of nature. And the magnitude of this issue is vast. For, given the generalisability of the example (to virtually *any de re* proposition), it turns out that, in order to accommodate *any* tricky case (e.g., *Can Obama be a table?*, *Can my desk be made of ice?*, and so on), we would need to impose indefinitely many singular propositions into the class of statements that govern nomic modality. How many exactly? A lot: any *true* (*de re*) predication *that we want* to come out as nomically necessary would need to be included.[5] I am however of the view that these true (singular) predications are not constitutive of nomic modality,

---

[4] All we need to assume (which can be granted for the sake of the example) is that it is not part of the meaning of *Socrates* that its referent is (must be?) a human.

[5] But no more than that. For instance, we presumably would *not* include the *true* predication about any organism's *mass* (because we want *mass* properties to count as contingent, both nomically and metaphysically). And this reveals the large degree of theoretical bias associated with this option: it embeds metaphysical modality into the characterisation of nomic modality. More on this in Section 2.5.

and thus thickening the characterisation of nomic modality in this way is not something I favour.

The alternative is to revise the received view about *extension*, and to embrace the idea that *Socrates is a dog* is nomically possible. For reasons that I shall unfold in Section 2.5 (partly inspired by Fine 2005), this is my recommended option. This option has a salient consequence: if we are not to revise *in addition* the (also) received view that it's metaphysically *im*possible for Socrates to be a dog, we would need to deny that nomic possibility implies metaphysical possibility, against what many seem to assume.[6] For the time being, I shall leave matters here but, as stated, we will return to this issue in Section 2.5.

Before moving on to the next modality, let me make a brief remark. One reason that nomic modality is a paradigmatic example of an alethic modality is the fact that it is characterised by means of a distinctively interesting set of truths: the laws of nature, which tell us how the world works. This makes it not only a paradigmatic example, but also a rather uncontroversial one; unlike perhaps a modality characterised by any random set of truths like, for instance, the first 100 truths I ever learnt. Our next example of alethic modality shares with nomic modality this feature of being a rather uncontroversial one, for analogous reasons. The philosophical issues that we will tackle in Section 2.5 largely concern the existence (or non-existence) of gerrymandered alethic modalities, somehow distanced from the nomic and metaphysical modalities.

2.4.2 Metaphysical Modality

A metaphysically interesting, and nowadays fairly uncontroversial, distinction is that between essential and accidental properties.[7] The importance of this distinction stems from the fact that essential properties are thought to be those that provide an answer to questions about an entity's *nature* (i.e., an entity's *identity*): what is it *to be* a given object? If we know that Greta Thunberg is not only human but also essentially so, this knowledge will help us understand better *what it is to be* Greta Thunberg, that is, what *being Greta Thunberg* consists in. As a first approximation (bear with me, as we will devote the whole of Section 3 to this type of modality), metaphysical modality can be character-ised as that modality that tracks the difference between the essential and the accidental properties of entities. Let me explain *why* it can be so characterised.

---

[6] I don't think this is a cost at all, but it certainly goes against the received *onion model* for salient alethic modalities, according to which the set of nomically possible worlds is properly included in the set of metaphysically possible worlds, which is in turn included in the set of conceptually possible ones. For a graphic illustration, see Figure 1.

[7] For approximations to the topic of essentialism, see Glazier's (2022) Element on *Essence* in this series, Robertson and Atkins (2020), and Roca-Royes (2011a, 2011b).

There are several essentialist theses that have been widely discussed in the literature and, among them, we will take in turn three of the most (historically) prominent: the Essentiality of Origins (EO), the Essentiality of Kind (EK), and Natural Kind Essentialism (NKE).[8] According to (EO), very crudely, origins – or origin properties, like *originating from x* – are essential to originated entities. Now, there is disagreement in the literature about how best to understand the claim that a given property, *P*, is essential to a given individual, *a*.[9] Here, we shall understand it as at least implying that *a* could not exist without being *P*. With this understanding, (EO) implies that my office desk, which originated (let's say) in hunk of wood *h*, cannot exist unless it originates from *h*. One can make a table from any other piece of wood but, if (EO) is true, the table that would come into existence in doing so would *not* be my office desk but a numerically different one. Analogously, coming from the zygote from which Aretha Franklin originated is, according to (EO), essential to her. If this is so, nowhere – in this world or any other possible world – is she to be found with different origins.

The (EK) thesis behaves similarly to (EO), but with different types of properties: namely, *sortal* properties, as they are often known in the literature. A working characterisation of this notion will suffice here: we understand by 'sortal property' of an object, *a*, a property that specifies the type of entity that *a* is in a distinctively robust metaphysical sense. Examples will help: *being human*, *being a table*, *being a number*, and *being an animal* are all taken to be (relatively) uncontroversial examples of sortal properties; unlike, for instance, *being happy*, *being a philosopher*, or *being my child's favourite car*. This working characterisation can now help us flesh out (EK). According to this essentialist thesis, the number two cannot be a triangle, or a kangaroo, as it is essentially a number, and this implies that it cannot exist in any form other than that of a number. Similarly, you cannot be a number, or a cat, or any *type* of entity other than a human.

In contrast to the two principles sketched so far, (NKE) is a thesis that implies that *natural kinds* also have essential properties. According to (NKE), if instances (or samples) of a given natural kind, *k*, have structure *x* (be this microphysical structure, biological structure, chemical structure, etc.), then it is essential to *k* that all its instances (or samples) have structure *x*. For example, the natural kind *water* would be essentially H_2O, and it would be essential to gold that it has atomic number 79.

---

[8] They are by no means uncontroversial theses and the literature is plagued with discussion about them, both by detractors as well as advocates. For a representative sample, see Brody (1967); Forbes (1985, 2001), Kripke (1972/1980), Mackie (1994, 2006), McGinn (1976), Robertson (2000), Salmon (1981), and Wiggins (1980).

[9] See Fine (1994), Wildman (2021), and (De 2020) for a tase of this discussion.

Now, as suggested above, to say that P is an essential property of a implies (so it is widely assumed) that, to the extent that a exists, the proposition that a *is* P is true. But it implies something stronger than that: it implies that it is *necessary* that a is P (to the extent that a exists) or, in other words, it implies that a *is* P *cannot* fail to be true.[10] I have been relying on this implication in the way I have sketched the three essentialist principles above. It is thus urgent to ask which sense of 'necessary' (or 'cannot') is intended here. And the answer, without further ado, is that this is the *metaphysical* sense. As such, *a being essentially P* implies that *it is metaphysically necessary that a is P* (whenever a exists at all). As anticipated, metaphysical modality can therefore be characterised as tracking the essential and the accidental properties of objects.

This way of introducing metaphysical modality is, I must warn you, *heavily* theoretically loaded. I'll make peace in Section 3 with those who are irritated by it, as that section is devoted to the *metaphysics* of metaphysical modality, and we'll see there the most salient alternative ways of understanding this modality. For the time being, the current characterisation will do.

Now, just a while ago (in Section 2.4.1) we saw that we can characterise nomic modality on the basis of the laws of nature. In a similar fashion, the suggestion (for now) is thus to characterise metaphysical modality on the basis of what we can call, by analogy, the *metaphysical laws* (henceforth 'ML'), where they are thought to be the set of essential truths. If we do so, the characterisation would be roughly as follows:

p is metaphysically necessary if and only if it (logically) follows from the elements in ML.
p is metaphysically possible if and only if it is (logically) compatible with all the elements in ML.

But the analogy with nomic modality can only go so far. To see why, I shall explore an issue that also emerged in the case of nomic modality. The exploration will reveal that, in the current case, the issue needs a different treatment. In Section 2.4.1 we assumed (presumably safely) that the laws of nature are all generalisations. By analogy, one would think of ML (the metaphysical laws) as generalisations too. Should we however take this to be the case? The three

---

[10] Theoretical neutrality is possible only up to a certain point and a qualification is in order here. There are some modal metaphysicians – known as *necessitists* – for which it is false that essentialist claims imply those necessity claims, *even* when taking into account the proviso about the object's existence. For a necessitist, Greta Thunberg might be essentially human and this might be compatible with there being worlds where she *exists* (in a robust, metaphysical sense) but lacks the property of *being human*, because she lacks the property of being concrete in the first place. See Linsky and Zalta (1994, 1996) as well as Williamson (2000, 2010, 2013, and 2016).

essentialist theses introduced above – (EO), (EK), and (NKE) – are certainly general principles and, if guided by this observation, one might be tempted to answer this question in the affirmative. However, as revealed below, there are reasons to think that certain *particular* propositions (or statements) – and not just general ones – must ineliminably be taken to belong to ML. (For this reason, in the metaphysical case, speaking of metaphysical *axioms*, rather than laws, is a better terminological choice.) Let us see some of these reasons.

We know – to stick to our example – that Greta Thunberg is human. Assuming (EK), it is essential to her to be so and, as such, in the metaphysical sense of the term, it is an *expected* result that her being human is a necessary fact (true in all worlds where she exists). In other words, in no possible world would it be the case that Greta Thunberg exists and is not human.

However, in a way that mimics the more contentious example that we saw in the case of nomic modality (about Socrates being possibly a dog), we can now raise a similar trouble-making question: is the proposition *that Greta Thunberg is a kangaroo* incompatible with the elements in ML? It is certainly not incompatible with the general principles (EK), (EO), or (NKE) per se, the reason being (as in Section 2.4.1) that these principles are generalisations of *conditional* statements. As a result, if ML is to include only general propositions – along the lines of (EO), (EK), and (NKE) – the above characterisation will deliver unintended results. For the possibility that Greta Thunberg could be a kangaroo is not ruled out, but this is (going by the majority view) a bad result: Greta Thunberg – and indeed any other human being – is assumed to be *essentially*, and thus *metaphysically necessarily*, a human being.[11] A fix is needed here to stop the unintended consequence from occurring.

Recall that, in the case of nomic modality, we identified two main options in relation to the example: to embrace, after all, that Socrates *can, nomically*, be a dog, or else to thicken our notion of nomic possibility. Although I expressed my preference for the former, both options are, as far as I can tell, theoretically open. In the case of nomic modality, one could argue, to some extent, that there isn't much at stake beyond labels. True enough – our working characterisation of nomic modality yields the result that Socrates could (in the nomic sense) be a dog. This might be surprising to those who unreflectively assumed (or inherited the view) that he nomically could not. Upon reflection though, why should *nomic* modality forbid it? Some theorists might insist on avoiding this result.

---

[11] That Greta Thunberg is essentially a human being is widely accepted among modal metaphysicians, but not universally. For a contemporary example of someone who thinks she's not, see Penelope Mackie's work; for instance, Mackie (2006), where she defends a minimalist view on essential properties, according to which there are very few such properties. The general point here, however, is not compromised by disagreement on the specific example.

For them, there might be ways of engineering a characterisation of nomic modality that avoids it.[12] By contrast, I see no strong reason to insist on avoiding that result: I don't see why it should matter to the *physical* order which entities fall under which categories. But regardless, the point is that any of these two theoretical reactions (to the unexpected result) appear to be characterising different *but equally legitimate* types of alethic modality. Which one we should label 'nomic modality' can thus be diagnosed as an unimportant linguistic decision.

Things are different in the metaphysical case, however. Remaining neutral here can be argued to be a poor option and, for the reasons that follow, we should see it as *misbehaviour* of any characterisation of *metaphysical* possibility if it yields the result that Greta Thunberg can, metaphysically, be a kangaroo; or, more generally, that she can metaphysically be anything that we *intuitively* think is contrary to her essence. Nothing depends on the specificity of this example.[13]

Why *should* this be seen as misbehaviour in the current case? We have introduced the notion of metaphysical modality, intuitively, as that alethic modality that tracks the possibilities for objects as constrained by their essential properties. What we are now facing is both the fact that Great Thunberg is (or so we are assuming) *essentially* a human being, but also the result that – with ML unsupplemented with *particular* facts – she could, metaphysically, be anything at all; a kangaroo, for instance. This result is in tension with grasping metaphysical possibility as constrained by essential facts; i.e., as tracking what it is to be Greta Thunberg. In other words: metaphysical modality speaks of *non-trivial* ranges of possibilities for entities, often referred to in the literature as *modal profiles*. And yet, these non-trivial ranges of possibilities largely escape metaphysical modality when characterised as above; i.e., when understanding ML as containing essentialist principles that are generalisations of conditional statements without being supplemented with the *true* particular, antecedent facts.

---

[12] Boris Kment (2006b, 2014), for instance, defines nomic modality in such a way that, effectively, to be a nomic possibility is to be a metaphysical possibility that also conforms to the laws of nature. I do not mean to suggest that Kment's reasons for defining nomic modality in this way include the kind of considerations explored here. The point is rather that, with such a thicker notion, *Socrates is a dog* comes out as nomically impossible, and there's no theoretical impediment to that characterisation. This thicker notion is also the one Williamson (2016, 462–3) operates with, and, in his case, the motivations *are* very much the sort of considerations to be found in this text.

[13] As mentioned in footnote 11, some essentialists (e.g., minimal essentialists) think that Greta Thunberg could be a kangaroo. As will be clear shortly, the current point survives this remark. So long as minimal essentialists *are* essentialists (albeit to a minimal degree), they too will encounter results that they should not welcome: for instance, that *Greta Thunberg could be abstract*.

This being so, the option of embracing the unintended results should be ruled out in this case. Once ruled out, we should thicken our characterisation of *metaphysical modality*. This thickening is indeed a simple way of reconciling the intuitive notion of metaphysical modality and the working characterisation: we should consider that ML is populated by certain (unconditional) particular propositions, as well as, perhaps, generalisations such as (EO), (EK), and (NKE). In particular, ML should include those particular propositions that are essentially true, such as *that Greta Thunberg is human*, that *Aretha Franklin originates from zygote z*, or that *my office desk's original material is hunk h*.[14] If we take ML to be so populated, the proposition that *Greta Thunberg is a kangaroo* indeed becomes incompatible with ML, as it clashes with the one about her being human along with (EK).[15]

I shall leave these matters here for the time being and wrap up this introduction to metaphysical modality with a brief comparative remark. What we have seen so far is that alethic modalities have in common that they can all be characterised in relation to a set of truths. Despite this common feature, there's some flexibility about what this set of truths can or should be taken to be (especially when characterising types of modalities for which we have a pre-theoretical conception). So far, we have seen two modalities related to two rather interesting sets: that of the laws of nature, which characterise how the world works, and that of the laws (or better, *axioms*) of metaphysics, which characterise the nature of things. These two sets of truths are not equivalent and, as a result, the modalities characterised in relation to them are not equivalent either. The example *Socrates is a dog* from Section 2.4.1 illustrates this non-equivalence, as (in my recommended move) it would turn out to be a possibility only in the nomic sense. Analogously, assuming along with many (and for the sake of the example) that at least some nomic necessities are not included in ML, some nomic necessities would turn out to be false in the metaphysical sense of 'can'.

But what further examples of alethic modalities can we provide?

---

[14] A question that I will leave open but the reader might wish to spend some time on is as follows. Once we have in ML all the particular propositions (the required ones to fix the current issue), does it become redundant to include *also* general statements such as (EO), (EK), and (NKE)? There is theoretical room for a positive answer as well as for a negative one. Whether we lean towards the positive or the negative might easily be influenced by reflecting on cases like the following. Consider a world, *w*, where all the *particular* essential facts are satisfied, but where, *in that world*, (EO) is false. In particular, let us assume that Greta Thunberg exists there and thus is human there (for *w* satisfies all *actual* essential facts), but let us assume that she is not, there, *essentially* human. If our intuitions suggest that *w* is metaphysically possible, we should want to *exclude* (EO) from ML; and we might want to include it if our intuitions suggest *w* is not possible.

[15] In Roca-Royes (2006, Sect. 2.3.1) the reader can find an exploration of how this problem is dealt with in the case of Peacocke's analysis of metaphysical modality – an analysis that participates in the current characterisation of the notion.

2.4.3 Conceptual Modality, and Others

Conceptual modality is another example of alethic modality. As its very name suggests, this modality is characterised on the basis of the set of conceptual, or analytical, truths – or an axiomatisation of them. How best to understand the notion of a conceptual truth is controversial.[16] For the purposes of this Element, we can adopt (along with the dominant recent literature) an epistemological conception of it. According to our working characterisation, a truth p is an analytical truth if and only if grasping the meaning of a thought or claim which expresses it suffices to put one in a position to know it (or justifiably believe it). (We might easily characterise *analytic falsity* along the same lines, but we won't need it here.) Consider, for instance, the proposition that *all bachelors are unmarried*. Anyone who understands it – and thus is competent with the concepts involved – can, merely on the basis of their understanding, come to determine its truth. This is not so with the proposition that *all tourist guides are nice to their groups*. In this latter case, even if the proposition were true, understanding it cannot by itself provide the sole basis for its rational acceptance. Of the two, therefore, only the former will make it into the set of conceptual truths; let's call this set 'CT'. With this in mind, conceptual modality (characterised next) is that modality with which to track these epistemic features:

p is conceptually possible if and only if it is (logically) compatible with all the elements in CT.
p is conceptually necessary if and only if it (logically) follows from the elements in CT.

It is easy to see that all conceptual truths turn out to be (quite trivially) conceptual necessities. An interesting question is whether conceptual truths are *also* metaphysically necessary and whether contingent analytic claims such as 'I am here now', permitted by their language's indexicality, suggest a negative answer. A more interesting question is whether conceptual modality is *genuinely* different from metaphysical modality. To *this* question we cannot give a theory-neutral answer, and I will address it later (to some extent) in Section 2.5.

A note of warning that I *do* need to stress now is the following. One might occasionally see conceptual modality, or a notion akin to it, taken to be an epistemic modality. For instance, this is (roughly) the sense in Kment's (2021)

---

[16] See Boghossian (1996) for a very influential, contemporary view on how to characterise the notion, and Williamson (2007) for reasons to be suspicious about this, as well as to its historical predecessors. And see Boghossian and Williamson (2020) for a recent insistence on this debate. See also Russell (2008, 2014) for an example of how to rescue the *metaphysical* conception of analyticity.

entry on 'Varieties of Modality', as well as in most of the literature on two-dimensional semantics.[17] There is an explanation for this, which we do not need to go into.[18] To prevent confusion, however, it is important that the reader be alerted that there is a limiting case of *epistemic modality*, within the epistemic ones, that can be assimilated to what we're now characterising as *conceptual modality* within the alethic ones.[19]

What about other types of alethic modalities? The following are often taken to be alethic modalities: mathematical modality, characterised on the basis of the set of mathematical truths; biological modality, characterised on the basis of the set of biological laws; psychological modality, characterised by the set of (human) psychological laws; logical modality, characterised by a set of inference rules (or corresponding axioms); and socio-economic modality, among others. What makes all of these somewhat natural examples of alethic modalities is the fact that the sets of truths on which they are characterised can all be taken to enjoy a law-like character (more or less artificially, depending on the cases).

As the reader will have noticed, I have omitted the characterisation of *logical* modality, despite its undeniable salience: this modality has been used to char-acterise all the modalities so far. I have omitted it because I intend a working notion of logical consequence (and consistency) to be sufficient for current purposes. And yet, to flesh it out a little bit, I shall join Bob Hale in taking this working notion to be a broad one, and leave it at that:

> Logical necessity is to be understood here in a broad sense. It is not restricted to those necessities which are substitution instances of logically valid sche-mata, such as $p \supset p$ or $\forall x((Fx \land Gx) \supset Fx)$, or their counterparts in natural languages, but includes also what are sometimes called analytic or conceptual necessities, such as 'Vixens are female' or 'Anything taller than the Eiffel Tower is taller than anything shorter than it'. (Hale 2013, 47)

---

[17] For leading representatives of two-dimensional semantics, see Chalmers (1996, 2004), Jackson (1998), and Kaplan (1989).

[18] The following remarks should suffice for current purposes. Take the notion (EP) of epistemic possibility as characterised in Section 2.2: the one characterised for a single individual. Consider now individual S of that characterisation, and assume them to satisfy the following two condi-tions: (i) S is an *ideal* thinker, in the sense that no (amount of) better reasoning could undermine any of S's judgements; and (ii) S has no empirical knowledge whatsoever beyond that which is required for S to be conceptually competent (relative to a given conceptual network, e.g., the conceptual network encoded in British English), but has instead all a priori knowledge afforded by their conceptual competence. Now, the property *epistemic possibility for S*, in the (EP) sense, is arguably at least coextensive with *conceptual possibility* in the way we characterised it here. See Kment (2021, Sect. 1) for a different way of assimilating the two properties.

[19] And yet things can get very messy very easily. Someone might object that conceptual modality should be assimilated to *analyticity* and that epistemic modality is to be assimilated instead to *aprioricity*, and that, since Kant's case for the *synthetic a priori*, we have known that these are not even coextensive properties. Going into this in detail will take us too far from our main focus and I shall leave things unrigorously approximate.

Here, I am more interested in a question that I postponed in Section 2.4.1: the question of how large the family of alethic modalities should (or can) be taken to be, which will be the focus of Section 2.5. To illustrate the controversy, let me conclude this section by introducing an extravagant *potential* example of alethic modality: Alaskan modality.

Alaskan modality is characterised by the set of truths about Alaska; let's call this set 'AT'. Despite its arguable extravagance, technically, the characterisation of Alaskan modality can be strictly analogous to that of any of the alethic modalities characterised above:

p is Alaskanly necessary if and only if it (logically) follows from the elements in AT.

p is Alaskanly possible if and only if it is (logically) compatible with all the elements in AT.

If we are to deny the existence of Alaskan modality, the reasons for this exclusion cannot therefore be the technical difficulties in characterising it (there aren't any such difficulties) or our difficulties in understanding that property (we do understand it). They will rather need to be *theoretical* reasons against our taking that property (whatever that might be) as a type of modality. For instance, one could make a non-ad hoc case that the truths in AT lack any law-like character. Some, however, and as we are about to see, do not require a law-like character of the truths which characterise a given, alethic modality and, consequently, such reasons would not persuade *them* to exclude these less typical examples from the realm of modalities.

2.5 Unification of Alethic Modalities?

It is now time to go deeper into the related family of issues we've been stocking up in Section 2.4. How many alethic modalities are there? This is now our central question. Let me start by noting that I have not been speaking of the characterisations of the different alethic modalities as *definitions* of them. This is purposeful. For we're now moving to a discussion about how many different kinds of modality there are, at a fundamental level. And, had I been speaking of the characterisations in Sections 2.2, 2.3, and 2.4 as definitions, I would have easily begged the question (against my intended neutrality) in favour of one side of this debate – the one which we shall call 'the *reductivist* relativist side'. Characterisations are, importantly, different from definitions. For instance, I can characterise the property of *being a cat* as *the fundamental kind of my pet*. And because I have only cats as pets (and in fact I have only one pet), that characterisation uniquely identifies the property of *being a cat*. Indeed, something is the property of *being a cat* if and only if it is the fundamental kind of my pet. With this characterisation, I am committing myself to the extensional equivalence between the two sides of the bi-conditional. But this commitment to the extensional equivalence doesn't commit me in turn to there being a *definitional* equivalence between the two. And, at least in this case, that is good, for I would rather deny the definitional equivalence: surely there is more to *being a cat* than being the fundamental kind of my pet!

Consider now all the characterisations in Section 2.4: the nomic, the metaphysical, the conceptual, etc. And consider the question of whether there is, in each case, a definitional equivalence between their two sides. As a first approximation, we can characterise the *reductivist relativists* in this debate as those who answer this question in the affirmative. By contrast, for the non-reductivists (whether relativist or not), among whom I count myself, there is more to *being a certain type of alethic modality* than satisfying the corresponding characterisations.

As we shall briefly see, one of the biggest selling points of the *reductivist* relativist is what we can refer to as 'the unification power'. Such a relativist has a readily available answer to the question what makes every kind of modality, precisely, a kind of *modality*: it is their all being relativised forms of logical modality. But at the same time, there's a feature of this reductionist stand, which we can label 'cheap proliferation', that, for many, myself included, is a 'not-buying' point. We will structure the discussion in this section around these two points, and we start with the former one: the unification power.

Jessica Leech is a prominent contemporary *reductivist relativist*, and she has defended this metaphysical stance in Leech (2016), where she neatly distinguishes it from the non-reductive relativist one. Following this, Hale and Leech (2017) have contributed further to our general understanding of the prospects and strengths (as well as weaknesses) of the different relativist projects. For they each have different metaphysical agendas, and one of the differences consists, precisely, in that it is only Leech who is a *reductivist* relativist. For Leech (but not for Hale) what they submit as good relativist *characterisations* of the different modalities *exhaust*, metaphysically, what these modalities *are*.

What are these relativist *characterisations*, on which they both agree despite their metaphysical discrepancy? The literature contains a very thorough, prece-dent discussion about what a relativist characterisation should look like. With the aim of providing a contemporary focus to the current Element, I shall simply set aside earlier proposals (and the problems they face) and jump directly to the relativist proposal as found in Hale and Leech (2017).[20] Here is, in maximal generality, their relativist proposal (Hale and Leech 2017, 14):

It is ϕ-necessary that p   iff $\exists q(\phi(q) \wedge \Box(q \rightarrow p))$,

where $\Box$ stands for *logical* necessity – and thus, '$\Box(q \rightarrow p)$' is to be read as 'p is a logical (necessary) consequence of q' – and where the variable ϕ (on the left-hand side) ranges over any potential type of relative necessity.[21] The following examples are all instances of this schema:

It is physically necessary that p   iff $\exists q(\pi(q) \wedge \Box(q \rightarrow p))$,
It is biologically necessary that p   iff $\exists q(\beta(q) \wedge \Box(q \rightarrow p))$,
It is technologically necessary that p iff $\exists q(\tau(q) \wedge \Box(q \rightarrow p))$,

where '$\pi(q)$', '$\beta(q)$', and '$\tau(q)$' abbreviate, respectively, 'it is a law of physics that q', 'it is a law of biology that q', and 'it is a law of technology that q'. According to the first instance, then, something (p) is physically necessary if and only if it logically follows from a law of physics.

Let's not be distracted by the fact that the form of Hale and Leech's relativist characterisations is very different from the one we've become used to so far: they include the existential quantification over certain types of propositions. The reason for this is that, without this change, any relative modality would *unavoidably* inherit the satisfaction of the S4 axiom ($\Box p \rightarrow \Box\Box p$) from the fact that logical modality satisfies it. And yet, it is desirable, they contend, not to impose the satisfaction of this principle.[22]

Regardless of form, unification, as anticipated above, is one of the biggest selling points of the *reductivist* relativist project. In the words of Hale and Leech (2017, 19), 'what drove that project' was precisely such a unificatory aim. That is, 'to show that, contrary to appearances, there is no need to recognize a variety of independent kinds of necessity – physical, mathematical, etc. – by showing that each of these ostensibly different kinds of modality may be fully explained using just one single kind of modality, such as logical modality' (Hale and Leech 2017, 20).

Unification, afforded here by the *reductive* relativist project, thus brings with it explanatory power. Let us look back at the general schema above: no matter

---

[20] This precedent discussion includes the earlier sections of Hale and Leech (2017), which the reader might want to check as a starting point. They constitute a beautiful summary of the discussion up to that point.

[21] Because of their metaphysical discrepancy, only Leech would be happy with replacing the biconditional in their characterisations with the symbol for the definitional equivalence, '=def', precisely as she does in Leech (2016).

[22] I cannot expand on this here, but this is one of the problems for earlier relativist proposals that is explained in Hale and Leech (2017).

which (relative) type of modality we're characterising – that is, no matter what we substitute for the variable ϕ – they are all characterised as relative on the basis of one and the same absolute modality: the logical one. When such a vast array of modalities are characterised, even *defined* (as per the reduction), in this way, an important feature that is shared by all of them is thereby identified and, ultimately, this shared feature can account for our taking them all to be kinds of *modality*. How successful is, however, this explanation?

To see a threat to it, note that there is a distinctive feature of the relativist characterisations proposed by Hale and Leech that deserves attention: namely, the fact that it rests, in each case, on an antecedent *understanding* of the *type of truth*, ϕ, relative to which a given kind of ϕ-necessity is being defined. To stick with the example of *physical* necessity, the definiens '$\exists q(\pi(q) \wedge \Box(q \rightarrow p))$' above says that p follows as a matter of logical necessity from *a law of physics*. This feature can be thought to threaten the unifying and explanatory power of the proposal. The reason is that, for such a definiens to work as intended, one needs to appeal to the notion of a physical law. In turn, for such appeal not to threaten the unifying power, this notion had better not involve a *sui generis* notion, and kind, of modality. But the concern is, precisely, that it might not avoid such *sui generis* modality. (And note that the reasoning is not specific to physical modality; rather, it generalises.) To uncover where the concern comes from, recall that, in Section 2.4.3, I mentioned that, typically, the kinds of truths relative to which one characterises an alethic modality all seem to enjoy a law-like character. To put the current concern in those terms, the worry is that, in each case, such a *law*-like character amounts to a type of *modal* force *not* to be assimilated to that of logical necessity (that of the '$\Box$' in the schema). And, if this is so, *logical necessity* on its own will not support the sought-after unification.

> Put bluntly, the objection says that by making essential use of operators so understood, the account simply gives up on the reductive explanatory aspiration . . . . This explanatory aim is completely undermined by our appeal to laws of physics, for example, because the notion of a law of physics itself involves the idea of physical necessity. (Hale and Leech 2017, 19)

It is largely around this issue that Hale's and Leech's metaphysical agendas come apart. Hale is less concerned about reduction and unification and is happy to settle for the less ambitious aim 'of achieving an improved understanding of the contrast between merely relative and absolute kinds of necessity. The achievement of that aim is in no way compromised by the irreducibility – if such it is – of the various kinds of putatively relative necessity to a single absolute necessity' (Hale and Leech 2017, 20).

For current purposes, what we need to stress is that the potential unification power is, by conception, a potential selling point for the *reductive* relativist, like Leech. As such, it is this type of relativist who needs to provide a response to the threat just identified. As we're about to see, this response can be tailored in tandem as a response to what we can label 'the problem of cheap proliferation'.

The source of this label traces back to Fine. In Fine (2005), he describes the reductive relativist as suffering from an unacceptable proliferation of modalities, and claims that there's nothing they can appeal to in order to explain the difference between, for instance, Physical modality and the gerrymandered Alaskan modality (Section 2.4.3). According to Fine, the former is non-trivial and the latter is trivial, cheap, and this distinction should not be lost.

This problem brings us back to the overarching question in this section: how many alethic modalities are there? Or, in other words, is there an alethic modality for any (whichever) set of truths? In the spirit of this complaint, one could say that it's just a by-product of the schema above that we can characterise Alaskan modality, but that there really isn't anything genuinely *modal* about it. And yet, when one (like Leech) takes the characterisations as *definitions*, in a reductive manner, there's no way of excluding these gerrymandered properties from being *modalities*.

How problematic, however, is this proliferation for the reductive relativist? By their lights, not much at all. Even Leech (2016) speaks of the many relative modalities as *cheap* when responding to Fine's challenge. And her doing so should not suggest that she shares with Fine his diagnosis of the proliferation as a *problematic* feature. On the contrary, she adopts the phrase 'cheap modality' but not its negative connotations. At a metaphysical level, Leech can't explain the difference *in kind* between a trivial and a non-trivial modality. But this is not deemed problematic because, by her lights, *there is none*. According to Leech (2016), there need not be – and there isn't – anything objectively special about the type of truth, ϕ, to which a given ϕ-necessity is relativised. Because of this, the door is open to define as many relative modalities as sets of truths, ϕ, one desires to consider. One can embrace all modalities, gerrymandered or not, because, metaphysically, modalities are indeed *cheap* and ontologically all on a par. Which relative modalities, among the vast many, *we* find interesting will depend on which sets of truths we find interesting. As a matter of fact, we find Physical modality, Mathematical modality, Biological modality, and a limited range of other modalities, more interesting than Alaskan modality or, to borrow Leech's (2016) own example, Argos modality – defined as relative to truths about items listed in the Argos catalogue. But, on her reductive framework, this difference in interest (by us humans) does not reflect any deep, metaphysical contrast between them.

In a nutshell, therefore, Leech's response to Fine's proliferation problem rests on denying a presupposition in Fine's complaint: the presupposition that some modalities are trivial and some are not. A reductivist relativist, like Leech, therefore, would *happily* bite the bullet of proliferation, and answer our overarching question in this section (about how many modalities there are) with something like 'as many as non-equivalent sets of truths there are, and no significant metaphysical distinction is to be made among them'.

As anticipated, this response constitutes, in turn, a response to the unification threat above: the vast many relative modalities are still, all of them, *just* relativised forms of logical modality. No *sui generis* modality sneaks in. Unification is thus achieved, despite the threat.

For many, however, embracing all these properties as *modalities* is unsatisfactory and indeed one of the main reasons for moving away from a *reductivist* relativist approach. What, then, are the alternatives? One alternative is clear from the above: *non-reductive* relativism. When one, like Hale, does not take reduction and unification as a goal in one's metaphysical agenda, one can insist (even when partaking in relativism) that any set of truths relative to which a (relative) modality is characterised must be such that its elements should have, precisely, a certain degree of modal force. (And when one is not attempting reduction, this appeal to a *sui generis* modal force need not be jeopardising.) If this is one's theoretical choice, the alleged Alaskan modality or Leech's Argos modality would easily be banned from being considered genuine modalities. Indeed, the intuitive contrast between them and, for instance, Physical modality is now explainable precisely in terms of the elements of LN – the set of laws of nature – having a certain degree of *sui generis* modal force, something that is absent in the case of the (now banned) gerrymandered modalities.

As far as we know, however, in giving up the reduction, non-reductive relativism also gives up the aim of unification; or, at the very least, it gives up the aim of *unifying by relativising*. In the remainder of this section, I shall focus on the two questions that are, in view of this, most dialectically relevant. First, what are the non-relativist alternatives? And, second, how do they fare with the prospects of unification?

In addressing these two questions, rather than covering a wide range of alternatives, I shall limit myself to *illustrating* answers to them by focusing on the contemporary work of Kment (2006b, 2014) and Fine (2005). These works are interesting in themselves, but they are also interesting in comparison to one another, as the following will make clear. (In Section 3, when we turn to the metaphysics of *metaphysical* modality in particular, we will consider other accounts (Thomasson's, for instance) whose consequences relate back to the issue of *unification*.)

Kit Fine (2005) opens up 'The Varieties of Necessity' with the question of unification, making it very clear from the outset that he doesn't think that full unification (even of alethic modalities) is possible:

> Necessity abounds. There are the necessary truths of logic, mathematics and metaphysics, the necessary connections among events in the natural world, the necessary or unconditional principles of ethics, and many other forms of necessary truth or connection. But how much diversity is there to this abundance? Are all necessary truths and connections reducible to a single common form of necessity? And if not, then what are the different ways in which a truth might be necessary or a necessary connection might hold? . . . It is the aim of this paper to show that diversity prevails. (Fine 2005, 235)

The diversity he settles for is tripartite, identifying three fundamental types of necessity, irreducible to one another: deontic, natural (i.e., physical, nomic), and metaphysical. In line with the above discussion, we will set aside for the time being the deontic type and focus instead on the two alethic ones: the natural and the metaphysical. In his exploratory remarks, Fine considers two different unification strategies. The first is the by now familiar *relativisation* (understood reductively) and the second, *restriction*. To briefly see why Fine considers these two types of alethic necessities as fundamental – and thus neither as definable in terms of the other – it is convenient to note that *relativisation* would allow us to define a broader type of necessity in terms of a narrower type, whereas *restriction* would allow us to define a narrower type of necessity in terms of a broader one.

What do we mean by this? Take, for instance, logical necessity in comparison with metaphysical necessity. It is standard to consider all logical necessities as metaphysical necessities, but not the other way around: *that Kit Fine is a person* would be a metaphysical necessity that fails to be a logical one. Because of this relation of *proper inclusion* – the logical necessities are properly included in the metaphysical ones – metaphysical necessity is taken to be broader than logical necessity. On this basis, we can either define metaphysical necessity in terms of logical necessity *by relativisation* (à la Leech), or we can define logical necessity in terms of metaphysical necessity *by restriction*. We are already familiar with the first strategy, and we know that Fine considers the 'cheap proliferation' feature of this strategy a reason (among others) to be unhappy with it. For him, *unification by restriction* has a better chance of succeeding. The specific way in which he envisions this strategy (in our current example) can be illustrated as follows. For Kit Fine, metaphysical necessity is the necessity that obtains in virtue of the identity (nature, essence) of *all* things. Because of this *universality*, there is a good sense in which metaphysical necessity is maximally broad, or absolute: namely, there isn't a necessity that is broader than it, in the specific sense of including *all* the metaphysical ones *plus* others.

Metaphysical necessity is, as a result, a good candidate on the basis of which to define narrower necessities by restriction. How would this go? Rather than considering the nature of *all* things, we'd consider instead the nature of a restricted type of things. Consider, for instance, only the nature of logical functions, and you get *logical* necessity; consider, instead, only the natures of mathematical entities, and you get mathematical necessity, etc. These narrower necessities are still, nonetheless, all grounded in the essences of things (that is, in the essences of more or less restricted collections of things). And because of this, 'each of them can be regarded as a *species* of metaphysical necessity' (Fine 2005, 237), allowing for a certain degree of unification: unification by restriction.

What, however, in the case of two necessities, such that none is broader/ narrower than the other? This, to cut Fine's story short, is what happens with the pair of *natural* (nomic) and *metaphysical* necessities and this fact, according to Fine, lies at the heart of their irreducibility to one another.

The following remarks explain why Fine takes metaphysical necessity to be neither broader nor narrower than natural necessity. Metaphysical necessity, obtaining as it does in virtue of the identity of things, is considered to be a *de re* necessity. At the fundamental level, there are *particular* identity facts – for instance, *that Kit Fine is a person* – that ground the necessities about those particulars – continuing with the example, *that Kit Fine is necessarily a person*. By contrast, natural necessity is, according to Fine, *de dicto*: the natural laws, from where natural necessity emerges, are instead generalisations. The follow-ing (largely overlooked) passage is worth quoting in full:

> Although I have emphasised the way in which natural necessities may out-run the metaphysical necessities, it seems to me that there is one respect in which this may not be true. For I am inclined to think that there are no distinctive *de re* natural necessities. Let us suppose that *x* and *y* are two particles and that it is a natural necessity that they attract one another (assuming, of course, that they exist!). Then it is plausible to suppose that this should follow from (a) its being a metaphysical necessity that each of the particles is of the kind that it is and (b) its being a natural necessity that particles of this kind attract one another. Thus the *de re* natural necessity will reduce to a *de re* metaphysical necessity and a *de dicto* natural necessity; and it might be thought that something similar should be true of any *de re* natural necessity or, indeed, of any form of *de re* necessity whatever. All forms of *de re* necessity (and of essence) will be fundamentally metaphysical, even though some forms of *de dicto* necessity may not be. (Fine 2005, 243)

What this means is that we can find certain generalisations – the natural laws – that (assuming their metaphysical contingency) would be natural but not metaphysical necessities, and we can in turn find certain particular facts – e.g., Kit Fine is a person – that would be metaphysical but not natural necessities, a result very much in line with our findings in Section 2.4.

None of them being strictly broader than the other, therefore, the natural and the metaphysical necessities generate a halting point when implementing the strategy of *unifying by restriction*. (And recall: this comes at a point where *unifying by relativisation* has already been ruled out, on grounds of the cheap proliferation with which Fine is unhappy.)

It is on this point that I find it very interesting to compare the work of Kit Fine with that of Boris Kment. Kment (2006b, 2021), like many modal metaphysicians, shares with Fine a hesitancy about the relativisation strategy: cheap proliferation is to be avoided as this would result in non-genuine modalities, in turn obscuring what genuine modalities have in common. This is how Kment phrases the concern (which, let it be recalled, would not worry a *reductive* relativist like Leech):[23]

> But what, on such a [relativist] view, is the commonality between nomic necessity and metaphysical necessity that makes them both kinds of necessity? Each of the two kinds of necessity is the property of being an analytic consequence of a certain set of propositions. But not every property of being a logical consequence of a certain set of propositions is a kind of necessity. What distinguishes those properties of this kind that are kinds of necessity from those that are not? The [relativist] account envisaged leaves us completely in the dark about the answer. (Kment 2006b, 271)

Unlike Fine, Kment is hoping for a larger unification. He praises accounts that, like Fine's, step away from reductive relativism and nonetheless manage to reduce – to three, in Fine's case – the number of fundamental modalities. But that would still be unsatisfactory according to Kment:

> The reduction of the various kinds of necessity to a small number of fundamental ones would be an important step towards the goal of a unified account of modality. But those who believe that there are several different fundamental kinds of necessity need to address another question: What is the common feature of these fundamental kinds of necessity that makes them all kinds of necessity? Why do they count as kinds of necessity, while other properties don't? (Kment 2021, Sect. 3)

Dialectically, it is important to note that if Kment were to succeed in answering these questions, then unification – one of the biggest selling points of the

---

[23] Lange (2005, 293–4) is similarly explicitly concerned about unification, reaching an account that shares several aspects with that of Kment's: 'different grades of necessity can be given a unified treatment, but without suggesting that *every* selection of some vocabulary to privilege or *every* logically closed set of truths corresponds to a variety of necessity'.

(reductivist) relativist – would not be a theoretical virtue exclusive to the relativist, making them lose abductive persuasion (on top of the problem, for many at least, that stems from cheap proliferation). As we shall see next, however, Kment's unification has some unexplained features, and there are reasons, congenial to Fine's considerations above, to doubt the naturalness of the unification he achieves. In presenting Kment's views, I avail myself (as he does) of the heuristic use of *worlds*. (More on worlds, briefly, in Section 2.7.)

Consider the set (or class) of logically consistent worlds, among which there is the actual world. This set is considered to form a *sphere* around the actual world. As is standard, a *sphere* is taken to be a subset of worlds that includes *all* worlds that are not further away than a certain distance from a given world, w, at the centre of the total space of worlds; and, for current purposes, the actual world, @, will always be the world at the centre.[24] As such, the claim that the logically consistent worlds form a sphere around the actual world means that any logically *in*consistent world would be further away than *all* logically consistent ones (see Kment 2014, Ch. 2.). According to Kment, the worlds in this sphere can be ordered by their degree of possibility, which relates to the inexorability of facts. Without needing to get too deep into this, we can take this inexorability to track the *modal force* of facts: the less easily a fact could have failed to obtain, the more secure, inexorable, it is: i.e., the greater its necessity. When we order the worlds in this sphere by their degree of inexorability, we realise – Kment contends – that the *nomically* possible worlds, too, form a sphere around the actual world, and so do the *metaphysically* possible worlds. Not only this: we also realise that, of the three spheres so far, the nomic sphere is the smallest one, and the logical one is the largest. What this means is that there is a point in the inexorability scale, v_n, below which *all* worlds are nomically possible and above which *all* worlds are nomically impossible; and there is also a further away point in that same scale, v_m, below which *all* worlds are metaphysically possible and above which *all* worlds are metaphysically impossible. Lastly, we would also find in the same scale the point of the logical sphere.

Now, in his book *Modality and Explanatory Reasoning*, Kment (2014) considers the outer sphere to be populated by the logically consistent worlds, just as we have done. This is a slight change from his paper, 'Counterfactuals and the Analysis of Necessity' (Kment 2006b), where he considered instead the set of conceptually coherent worlds. We don't need to worry about this change. As mentioned in Section 2.4.3, we're resting in this Element on a working notion of logical necessity broad enough to include conceptual (analytical)

---

[24] What determines the distance among worlds is a controversial topic we cannot spend time on here. Those interested can read, comparatively, Lewis' (1973) foundational book *Counterfactuals* and Kment's (2006a, 2014) alternative approach.

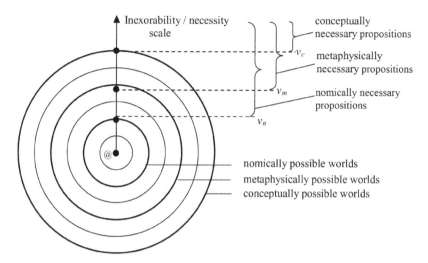

Figure 1 Kment's inexorability scale and system of spheres.
Source: Kment (2006b, 259)

necessities, and it will not harm this presentation if we do not distinguish them. If we don't, we can graphically illustrate the above, by means of Figure 1.

In terms of necessities, this image represents that, among the nomic, the metaphysical, and the conceptual ones, the nomic is the least inexorable, followed by the metaphysical one, with the conceptual being the most secure of the three types: you could more easily violate a natural law than a metaphysical one, but you can more easily violate a metaphysical law than a logical one.

It is the *existence* of these points, v_n, v_m, and v_c, on the *same* scale that, according to Kment, makes logical, metaphysical, and nomic modality all *species* of the same *genus*. With it, Kment achieves a salient unification, one that Fine had aborted: namely, subsuming nomic and metaphysical modality under one same genus. What makes these two modalities types of *modalities* is that they both identify points in the inexorability scale. In turn, it is the *non-existence* of corresponding points for the notions of biological, technological, epistemic, mathematical, or practical necessities (among others) which makes Kment not count them as further species of the same genus.[25] Instead, for this other battery of modal notions, Kment considers, much like Fine does, the option of defining them by restriction or relativisation. And in so doing, Kment considerably widens the unification power of his account.

---

[25] See Kment (2006b, 263) for his reasoning in support of this non-existence result.

Should we, however, be happy with the unification that Kment achieves? In particular, should we be happy that nomic necessity is a species *of the same genus* as metaphysical necessity? It would not have escaped the reader that, on Kment's account, and contrary to Fine's, nomic necessity is *strictly broader* than metaphysical necessity. And conversely for the possibilities: the nomically possible worlds are properly included in the metaphysically possible worlds. Crucially, it is only because of this that Kment is able to identify point v_n in the inexorability scale, allowing him to declare nomic modality as a species of the same genus as that of metaphysical modality. But the ultimate reason why he achieves this result is, I contend, because he has stipulatively embedded metaphysical necessity into nomic necessity:

> (DN) A proposition is nomically necessary iff *it is true throughout the sphere around actuality that contains the worlds that match actuality with respect to the metaphysical laws* and which have the same natural laws as actuality. (Kment 2014, 189; my italics)[26]

The italics on the right-hand side of (DN) correspond to Kment's definition of metaphysical necessity. It follows from Kment's definition of *nomic necessity* that nomically necessary propositions are those *metaphysically* necessary propositions that meet an *additional* condition: namely, not violating any natural law. This, as seen above, opens up a theoretical possibility that Fine considers unavailable: namely, construing one necessity in terms of the other, by restriction or relativisation.

But why this definition? Why include the metaphysical laws (or axioms) as constraints upon nomic modality? We know the terms in which Fine would disagree with Kment: nomic modality has to do with certain generalisations, the natural laws. In requiring, by definition, that nomically possible worlds also be metaphysically possible, what is being defined – a Finean could complain – is rather the conjunctive property of being both metaphysically *and* nomically necessary. Should we fight over labels? Let's not, as we didn't in Section 2.4 either. Even if we allow the label 'nomic necessity' to be invested in this way, the following concern remains. There is a legitimate notion of alethic necessity, let's call it 'nomic* necessity', that is not conjunctive in that way (thus simpler? more fundamental?), that has to do with the laws of nature, and such that the nomically* possible worlds *do not* form a sphere around the actual world. Instead of forming a sphere, the set of nomically* possible worlds is the union of the *sphere* of (Kment's) nomic worlds plus a *shell* hovering over the sphere of metaphysically possible worlds. (A *shell*, in contrast to a sphere, is to be understood as a subset of

---

[26] See also Kment (2006b, 270) for the analogous definition.

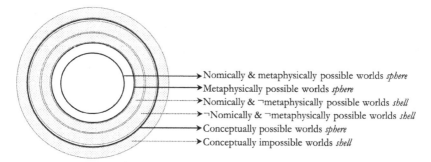

Figure 2 Roca-Royes' system of spheres and shells.
Source: Roca-Royes (2012, 153)

worlds that includes *all* worlds that are neither closer than a certain distance nor further away than a certain other, longer distance from the centred world, in our case, @. A shell, but not a sphere, therefore, has a *spheric* empty cavity.)

All the worlds in that shell satisfy the laws of nature but in metaphysically *im*possible ways: in some of them, for instance, Socrates is a dog; in others, my desk is made of cast iron instead of wood, etc. Apart from these *metaphysical* oddities, these worlds are *physically* far from extraordinary: Socrates barks in all such worlds where he is a dog. Now, nomic* necessity cannot, by Kment's lights, be taken as a species of the same genus as metaphysical modality: for the distribution of its worlds means that there is no point in the inexorability scale below which all worlds are nomically* possible and above which all worlds are nomically* impossible. As a result, this property, regardless of labels, threatens the unification attempt. Furthermore – and now I *am* fighting for the label – nomic* necessity is not just a robust kind of necessity. It is also, I contend, the kind of necessity that our folk notion of natural necessity is tracking: it doesn't matter to the physical order which individuals fall under which categories. The alternative (arguably Finean) graphic is thus as in Figure 2.

Nothing in the above is conclusive, but it does alert us to the point that we should be cautious about the prospects of achieving a unified, non-relativist account of alethic modalities. (This issue will emerge again in Section 3.5.)

2.6 Broader Unification?

The previous section focused exclusively on alethic modalities and, even when so restricted, the discussion has already proved complex and far from conclusive. To complicate things further, let's not lose sight of the other families of modalities – the epistemic ones and the deontic ones. For what we say about them might have an impact on the discussion we've just had in Section 2.5, in one of at least two ways. First, Fine, for instance, thinks that *normative* necessity is a fundamental kind of necessity, and one that can subsume neither the nomic nor the metaphysical type. One might want to scrutinise the reasons for this. If one agrees with them, the fact that metaphysical and nomic necessities cannot be unified *either* could easily be seen as having less relevance: once we accept that there is in any case no *one* fundamental necessity, how concerned should we be if there are three rather than two of them?

In the other direction, we know that the friends of (reduced) relativised modalities have unification as one of their biggest selling points. In Section 2.5 we explored the relativist strategy but, again, only focusing on alethic modalities. But turning our attention to the epistemic and normative modalities might reveal the achieved unification – *within* the alethic modalities – to be less of a big selling point than initially thought. For, if it turned out that the epistemic and the deontic families cannot be subsumed under the relativisation strategy, how much unification does this strategy really achieve? This (potentially) decreased value of the relativist approach would come on top of the cheap proliferation feature of alethic modalities, considered by many (as we have seen) to be a problematic one, even if dialectically inert.

A lot, then, is still left to be scrutinised about the unification agenda. For now, it suffices, as we have just done, to identify the dialectical relevance of these remaining issues. To date, Leech (2020) has walked some distance into exploring the prospects of extending reductive relativism to other families of modality, such as the epistemic and the normative, thus providing some reasons for optimism (even if moderate by her very own lights) that a wider unification might be workable.

The unification aspirations of some theorists will become salient again later on (in Section 3), when we focus on the metaphysics of metaphysical modality. Indeed, unification (or non-unification) agendas are not neutral on the *metaphysics* of the different types of modalities. Far from it, they can be seen as attempts to homogenise (or else leave heterogeneous) the metaphysics of the seemingly different families of modalities. As hinted at here, Leech's unification agenda goes hand in hand with a reductive relativist approach. And, as we shall see in Section 3.5, Amie Thomasson's *modal normativism* is, in the first instance, the project of understanding *metaphysical* modality as a type of normative (deontic) modality. But Thomasson's wide-scope project is much more ambitious than this: she aims to unify *all* alethic modalities by understanding them all as normative (Thomasson 2007, 136–7). Before turning to the metaphysics of metaphysical modality, however, there are two further issues to consider (Sections 2.7 and 2.8), still under the *general* phenomenon of modality.

2.7 Analyses of Modalities in Terms of Worlds

There is a widespread practice in philosophy of providing truth-conditions for modal claims (or propositions) in terms of possible worlds. Some authors who endorse an analysis of modality in terms of possible worlds hold that the analysis is reductive, David Lewis (1986) being the chief example. Others may be happy with the analysis as an extensional one, but not as a definitional one. And others think that no notion of *possible world* is suitable to mount even an extensionally adequate analysis of modality upon it, and yet they might nonetheless recognise the heuristic value of speaking of modality in terms of possible worlds; witness the widespread practice of doing this. In this section, we will consider the main rubric of the analysis and how it behaves in relation to the various types of modalities distinguished in the sections above.

In maximally general terms, the analysis is as follows:

$\Box$p is true if and only if p is true in all possible worlds.

$\Diamond$p is true if and only if p is true in some possible world.

According to the analysis – which is in fact a schema – 'necessarily' behaves like a universal quantifier over possible worlds and 'possibly' as an existential one. Consequently, to the extent that we're committed to at least the extensional adequacy of such analysis, and to the extent that we in turn believe that, for instance, *the sun could shine in Stirling today*, we're committed to there being a possible world where it is sunny today in Stirling. Endorsing the analysis (as more than a heuristic), therefore, incurs an ontological commitment: namely, to possible worlds.

This ontological commitment has generated a lot of literature over many years. Among the questions raised, there is the issue of the nature of possible worlds: what kind of entities would they be (or are they)? There is also the question whether they would be fit to reduce modality (or certain kinds at least) to them. If they were, our overall theory of the world would be able to dispense with *primitive* modal notions (of those kinds, at least), as we would be able to analyse them in non-modal terms. And there is also the question whether the set (or class) of possible worlds that one accepts into one's ontology is large enough for one's theoretical purposes.[27]

---

[27] See David Lewis (1986) for the paradigm example of *concretism*. See Armstrong (1989), Peacocke (1999), Plantinga (1974), Sider (2002), and Stalnaker (1976) as examples of so-called *ersatzism*. See Rosen (1990), and Armstrong (1989), as examples of *fictionalism*. For introductory literature on the metaphysics of possible worlds, see deRosset (2009a, 2009b), Divers (2002), Melia (2003), and Yagisawa (2009). And for examples of *modalism* – the view against analysing modal operators as quantifiers over possible worlds – see Forbes (1989), Jubien (2009), and Bueno and Shalkowski (2009, 2015). Lastly, Borghini (2016) provides an excellent critical introduction to the metaphysics of modality that places emphasis on how the

When it comes to analysing modality reductively, David Lewis (1986) uses possible worlds to analyse, in the first instance, what I shall call 'combinatorial modality', and he then analyses other modalities derivatively. *Combinatorial modality* is to be understood as that modality that tracks ways in which matter and fundamental properties can occupy (be distributed over) a space–time system. This is importantly silent on *de re* matters (more on this in Section 3.1) and, as such, it will be convenient to understand combinatorial modality, for now, as defined for *purely general propositions* only.[28] For any purely general *p*:

$\Box p$ is true if and only if p is true *in* all possible worlds.
$\Diamond p$ is true if and only if p is true *in* some possible world.

For Lewis, possible worlds are concrete in the same sense in which *our world* (the actual world) is concrete. They are spatio-temporally unified, and also spatio-temporally isolated from one another.[29] And there's a *plenitude* of them: there are at least as many of them as (qualitative) ways our world (and any other concrete world) could be. This plenitude is a necessary condition for the *at least extensional* adequacy of the account: if not all possibilities for our world were witnessed by some world, the left-to-right direction of the $\Diamond$-analysis above would fail. (For instance, if there could be talking donkeys but no world contained talking donkeys.) Lewis also takes it to be the case that every (qualitative) way some world is is a possible way for our world to be, with which he also secures the right-to-left direction of the account. Once the extensional adequacy is guaranteed, Lewis argues that his *concretism* is the only way in which one can hope the possible worlds analysis of (combinatorial) modality to be *reductive*.[30]

---

debate on possible worlds has progressively faded away in favour of a debate on possibilism *vs.* actualism.

[28] One might feel inclined to use 'metaphysical modality' ambivalently, to include combinatorial modality too (I myself sometimes do). I have been rightly pressed by a referee, however, that this is confusing, for a number of good reasons. Among them, metaphysical modality, as I used the label in Section 2.4.2, is distinctively *de re*. By contrast, *combinatorial modality* as introduced here is distinctively *de dicto*. It is true nonetheless that Lewis' worlds are 'first-class metaphysical possibilities' (in a way reminiscent of what Chalmers (2002, 165) claims for his primary-possible worlds). And yet, these (first-class) metaphysical possibilities are *purely qualitative* and, for this reason, to avoid unnecessary confusion, it is advantageous not to use the label 'metaphysical' to refer to Lewis' target modality. (See Roca-Royes (2020, Sect. 2) for more on the Lewisian distinction between qualitative and *de re* ways for a world to be.)

[29] Where 'spatio-temporal' should not be interpreted strictly but *analogically*: allowing for 'space–time' systems that differ from ours (see Lewis (1986, 76, fn. 55)).

[30] Lewis' (1986) *On the Plurality of Worlds* is a book-length abductive argument for this claim.

Are these (Lewisian) worlds, however, enough for our theoretical goals? Do we not need *im*possible worlds in addition? The answer depends on what exactly our theoretical goals are, and how much theoretical unity we're hoping for. Lewis can go a long way with his concrete worlds. He certainly can't afford any *combinatorially* impossible worlds (the extensional adequacy of the account, or else its reductiveness, would be jeopardised if there were some). And yet, some of his worlds will be impossible in other senses of the term. For instance, the nomic one: if, as many think, the natural laws of our world are (combinatorially) contingent, then there are Lewisian worlds where they are false. Any such world would be (relative to us) *nomically impossible*. As such, an analysis of nomic modality (in terms of worlds) is available to Lewis *by restriction*:

$\square_N$p is true if and only if p is true in all worlds *that share the actual worlds' laws of nature.*

$\lozenge_N$p is true if and only if p is true in some world *that shares the actual worlds' laws of nature.*

Generalising, Lewis could use his *concrete* worlds to straightforwardly analyse, by restriction, those modalities, *i*, such that the set of *i*-possible worlds is included (properly or not) into the set of his possible worlds.[31]

With the help of *counterpart theory* (as we will see more extensively in Section 3.1), Lewis can also, albeit less straightforwardly, provide an analysis of what he calls *de re* modality (a modality intimately linked to essentialism and, as such, much closer to what we referred in Section 2.4.2 as 'metaphysical modality').

Complications arise when it comes to analysing modalities, *j*, whose set of possible worlds outruns, or *would* outrun, the set of Lewisian worlds. For in that case, the most straightforward analysis *that Lewis could afford* with his concrete worlds would fail. The analysis would be something like this:

$\square_j$ p is true if and only if p is true in all possible worlds.

$\lozenge_j$ p is true if and only if p is true in some possible world.

And because the concrete worlds that the analysis can avail itself of are all combinatorially possible (the ontological commitments of Lewis' theory don't go beyond them), there will be cases of *p*'s such that *p* is (intuitively) *j*-possible and yet there isn't any world where it is true. Thus, the analysis would fail left-to-right for *possibility-j*. Conversely, there will be cases of *p*'s such that *not-p* is

---

[31] In the case of nomic modality, some philosophers, notably those of a Shoemakerian tradition, would object to the 'properly'. See Shoemaker (1980, 1998) for some foundational arguments in favour of the metaphysical necessity of the natural laws.

true in all concrete worlds and yet *not-p* fails to be (intuitively) *j*-necessary. Thus, the analysis would fail right-to-left for *necessity-j*.

Given that Lewis' combinatorial modality is already very liberal (after all, it covers *all* ways in which a *possible* space–time system might be filled in), it is not easy to find natural *j*-examples among alethic modalities. Doxastic modalities, on the other hand, are a source of such examples. They have been found problematic for Lewis given that a single subject might (perhaps inadvertently) believe both that *p* and that *not-p*. These doxastic cases are problematic because all combinatorially possible worlds are logically possible: logic puts a limit on how space–time can be filled in. To deal with these cases, less simple manoeuvres would need to be engineered to adequately analyse such modalities with the ontology available. For instance, as has been suggested, one could use *classes of worlds* instead of *worlds*, or a mixture between concrete and abstract worlds.[32] The literature, however, contains doubts that extensional adequacy can be achieved.[33]

Despite the theoretical benefits of Lewisian Concretism (see Lewis (1986, Ch. 1)), his *concretism* has been a severe *no-no* for most contemporary metaphysicians of modality.[34] Other, related, reasons can be summed up with the phrase 'combinatorial modality should not be the target modality.[35]

Moving away from Lewis' concretism, the most salient alternative concerning the nature of possible worlds is *abstractism* – the family of views that Lewis labelled, less sympathetically, 'ersatzism'. This family is unified, as the name reveals, by their taking possible worlds to be abstract entities. And while this agreed abstractness still allows for disagreement about their specific nature, *linguistic abstractism* is arguably the prevalent option. When it comes to analysing *metaphysical* modality (understood as introduced in Section 2.4.2), a linguistic possible world, *w*, would be a set of sentences or propositions such that: (i) it is consistent; (ii) for any sentence or proposition, *p*, either *p* or its negation, but not both, belongs to *w*; and (iii) all the elements that belong to LM – the metaphysical axioms – belong to *w*.[36] Lewis (1986) makes a very

---

[32] See Lewis (1986, Sect. 1.4) for ways of doing this. And see Berto (2010) and Kiourti (2010) for very thorough explorations of the *hybrid strategy*.

[33] For a recent discussion of Lewis' analysis of doxastic content, see Reinert (2013).

[34] An important exception in this regard is Alastair Wilson. In *The Nature of Contingency* (Wilson 2020) he defends an Everettarian interpretation of quantum mechanics, its (theoretical) services in analysing modality, and how it has the resources to avoid problems (both metaphysical and epistemological) that afflict Lewis' early modal realism. Knobe, Olum, and Vilekin (2006) endorse a similar ontology although, in their case, the metaphysical commitment is of a more exploratory nature.

[35] Kripke's (1972/1980, 45) famous Humphrey Objection can be understood as an expression of exactly this reticence.

[36] Both in (ii) and in (iii) we could say 'belong/s to *w or is/are implied by some element in w*', in case we want to allow for *axiomatic* worlds. Axiomatic worlds would include a given *p* but not (necessarily) all its logically equivalent sentences (or propositions). And, analogously, for pairs

strong case that any abstractist account would need to sacrifice *reductive* aspirations: with any such account, primitive modality will sneak into the theory somewhere. For instance, the indispensable notion of *consistency* in (i) above is modal, and such modality is not *definitionally* analysable (without circularity) by means of (i)–(iii).

Concerning this, Fine's (1994) ontological divorce between the essential and the modal has been understsood by some as giving the linguistic abstractist enough reductive power; an excellent example here is Peacocke (1999).[37] But even if one were to agree with Lewis about the poor prospects of *reductive abstractism*, modal metaphysicians would often be ready to sacrifice reductiveness – *if need be* – for the sake of other virtues such as believability (in its adequacy).[38]

In this context, the following remarks are relevant. Daniel Nolan (1997, 2013) is salient as a source of theoretical reasons why one might want to endorse an ontology of (metaphysically or combinatorially) *im*possible worlds. Many of these reasons refer to theoretical benefits that are unavailable when admitting only (combinatorially) *possible* worlds.[39] Now, if we – for these or other reasons – are realist about (combinatorially) *im*possible worlds, then abstractism about *them* is arguably the most natural approach. (What kind of entity would a *concrete*, yet combinatorially *impossible* world be?[40]) And once we are abstractist about (combinatorially) impossible worlds, then, presumably, for parity reasons, abstractism *too* about possible worlds is the most natural approach.[41] This reason for 'abstractism across the board' would come on top of the independent reasons one might already have to stay away from Lewisian Concretism.

Those leaning towards abstractism irrespective of the above reasoning might still wish to accommodate Nolan's recommendation about accepting an ontology of *im*possible worlds. It should be good news for them that they can do so in

---

of sentences or propositions, p and q, on the one hand, and their logical consequences, on the other, $p{\wedge}q$, $\neg(\neg p \vee \neg q)$, etc.

[37] With the qualification that Peacocke remains neutral about the analysis of modality in terms of possible worlds. He thinks that, on the basis of Fine's work, his account *might* support a reduction of the modal to the essential (Peacocke 1999, 148).

[38] The *incredulous stare* against concretism (Lewis 1986, Sect. 2.8), although not an argument in itself, certainly prompts methodological issues (favouring abstractism) concerning the justificatory limits of the *serviceability* of a theoretical hypothesis (or, more rigorously, on the limits of the strength of arguments which rest on it).

[39] See also Kment (2006b, 2014) and Berto (2010) for more reasons and theoretical uses of impossible worlds.

[40] See Yagisawa (1988) for a way of taking up the challenge of answering this question.

[41] This reasoning indeed rests on the so-called Parity Thesis (Berto and Jago 2018). We've seen, however (footnote 32), that a hybrid account is a theoretically open possibility too, so the reasoning might not necessarily feel persuasive.

a far from extravagant manner. For instance, if abstract (metaphysically) possible worlds are understood as being regulated by (i)–(iii) above, then any set of sentences (or propositions) that doesn't satisfy some of these three conditions can be taken as a metaphysically impossible world. Ontologically, a possible and an impossible world would be on a par: they both would be sets of sentences or propositions. Not only does the extension not need to involve ontological extravagance, it wouldn't involve ontological *inflation* either. Regardless of whether we decide to put them to theoretical use or not, there *already are* sets of sentences (or propositions) which fail to satisfy some of (i)–(iii); or, at any rate, there are *by the lights of* anyone who already accepts an ontology of *possible* worlds understood in that way, and thus the *extension* to impossible worlds doesn't involve inflation.

Such a plenitude of worlds allows for a straightforward possible worlds analysis of any alethic or deontic modality, *i*. The schema is the familiar one:

$\Box_i$ p is true if and only if p is true in all *i*-possible worlds.
$\Diamond_i$ p is true if and only if p is true in some *i*-possible world.

In the case of epistemic (and doxastic) modalities, the analyses would be analogous, but with explicit mention of the subject(s) to whom they are relativised.

Going back to something we discussed in Section 2.5, I shall wrap up this section with a remark on the prospects of *reductively* analysing the target modalities in terms of abstract possible worlds: it is precisely the use of the notion *i* on the right-hand-side of the analysis (i.e., on the analysans) that would threaten, unless such mention is eliminable, the *reductiveness* of these analyses.

2.8 Modality *De Dicto* and Modality *De Re*

To end this first part of the Element, I turn now to a distinction that I've merely used so far (mostly in Section 2.5) but that deserves more prominent attention. This is the distinction between modality *de dicto* and modality *de re*.[42] Let me start by requoting a passage from Fine (2005, 243): 'All forms of *de re* necessity (and of essence) will be fundamentally metaphysical, even though some forms of *de dicto* necessity may not be.'

A guiding aim of this section is to come to understand – better than we did in Section 2.5 – the reasons to hold this claim, and to bring out, to some extent, its truth.

---

[42] The *de re/de dicto* distinction has well-known applications outside modality too. However, this section is not about the distinction in general but rather, more narrowly, about the distinction within modality.

The task is not straightforward. A prior difficulty is that of characterising the difference between modality *de re* and modality *de dicto*, so that we are clear about what the claim says in the first place. This is difficult because the literature contains several ways of understanding the distinction which are not always equivalent.[43] We are thus facing two different tasks that nonetheless have to be carried out in tandem: we want (i) to find agreement with Fine's claim, but on (ii) an understanding of the distinction between modality *de re* and modality *de dicto* that is not too removed from our intuitive grasp of it. What we don't want is the claim's truth to rest on an artificial sense of the distinction.

The etymological is perhaps the standard way of informally characterising the distinction, and it's the one that I will use to measure my success in relation to task (ii). On this characterisation, modality *de dicto* refers to the phenomenon of propositions or sentences being necessarily, possibly, or contingently true or false. The *bearers* of *de dicto* modality are thus truth-apt entities, and this feature gives modality *de dicto* its name, which comes from the Latin *dictum*, for sentences or propositions (or, more generally, truth-apt entities). An example of *de dicto* modality thus results from applying the notion of *necessity* (or *possibility*, or *contingency*) to, for instance, the proposition *that lions don't fly*, the result being the proposition *that necessarily, lions don't fly*. By contrast, on the same characterisation, modality *de re* refers to the phenomenon of *entities* bearing properties in different modes: necessarily, possibly or contingently. We know for instance that Socrates bears (i.e., instantiates, exemplifies) the property of *being human*. The thought that Socrates has this property as a matter of necessity – i.e., *that Socrates is necessarily human* – would therefore be a *de re* modal thought, which refers to the fact that *being human* is necessary *of* Socrates.[44]

There is something of this intuitive grasp of the distinction, though, that creates noise and needs clarification. Consider the proposition *that Socrates is human*. This is as much a truth-apt entity as the proposition *that lions don't fly*. If we now apply *necessarily* to it, we get *Necessarily, Socrates is human*, and we would be inclined, as per the above, to count this modality as *de dicto*. But is it? The claim 'Necessarily, Socrates is human' doesn't seem to differ in truth-conditions, and hardly in meaning, from 'Socrates is necessarily human', and

---

[43] For examples of different characterisations as they have been captured in the literature, see Gallois (1998) and Cieśluk (2010).

[44] Sometimes, *de re* modality – unlike *de dicto* modality – is understood as implying the existence of *modal properties*. On this understanding, we would attribute the modal property of *being necessarily human* to Socrates, rather than attributing to him the *non-modal* property of *being human* and adding to such attribution the further claim that it is *of necessity* that Socrates has that property. We don't, for current purposes, need to take that step.

yet the latter is taken (as per the above too) to involve modality *de re*. How can they (or should I say 'it') involve different types of modalities?

To clarify this, let me note that this intuitive characterisation is often captured in syntactic terms. Roy's way of doing this is particularly helpful here to pre-empt the noise just identified:

> [T]his distinction corresponds to a formal one according to which a sentence (is *de re* and) expresses a proposition that is *de re* iff it *has a proper name inside the scope of a modal operator*, or a variable in the scope of a modal operator not bound by a quantifier in the operator's scope; and a sentence (is *de dicto* and) expresses a proposition that is *de dicto* iff it is not *de re*. On this basis, 'Possibly Quine is a rock' and 'There is a man such that possibly he is a rock' with their natural symbolizations, '◇Rq' and '∃x(Mx & '◇Rx)' are *de re*. 'Necessarily whatever is green is colored' with its natural symbolization, '□∀x(Gx ⊃ Cx)' is *de dicto*. (Roy 2000, 60; my italics)

There are two things to note from this: first, the intuitive distinction between modality *de re* and modality *de dicto* is an exclusive one and, consequently, we don't want 'Necessarily, Socrates is human' to be taken as both *de dicto and de re*.[45] Second, this proposition is taken to be *de re* (only) and this is how it should be when precisifying the intuitive grasp of the distinction. Indeed, much in line with the suspicion that 'Necessarily, Socrates is human' doesn't differ in meaning from 'Socrates is necessarily human', the two claims are symbolised in exactly the same way; namely, □Hs (where 'H' stands for *being human* and 's' is a constant for Socrates).

We can now see that, as a result, modality *de dicto* applies to dictums *of a purely general type*; that is, to sentences or propositions with no reference to particular individuals.[46] What this means is that *de dicto* modality tracks necessary (or contingent, or impossible) relations among the distribution of properties and relations, whereas *de re* modality tracks modes in which entities have properties (or stand in relation to other entities).

With this, I take myself to have achieved task (ii) above; namely, to have reached an understanding of the distinction between modality *de re* and modality *de dicto* that is not removed from our intuitive understanding. This is indeed,

---

[45] By 'an exclusive distinction' we mean that nothing can be both. That the *de re/de dicto* distinction is exclusive is generally accepted. Roy is certainly not alone in drawing the distinction by defining only one of the two modalities – in Roy's case, *de re* modality – and by stating that the modality is *otherwise* of the other type – in Roy's case, *de dicto*. See. for instance, Cresswell and Hughes (1968, 184) and Nelson (2019).

[46] For clarity, note that proper names are not needed for reference to particular individuals. As Cieśluk (2010, 84) remarks: 'By enlarging the range of rigid designators beyond proper names one can read the descriptions ['the most famous French General'] in two ways: referential and attributive. The first one refers to the *de re* interpretation[,] the second to the de dicto interpretation.'

I believe, the prevalent understanding. As we shall see in Section 3, this is also the understanding that guides Wang's classification of the different accounts of metaphysical modality as *de dicto first* or *de re first*. (More on this very soon.)

But before coming to this, what about task (i)? Is this understanding of the distinction one with which to understand better the reasons behind Fine's opening quote, as well as to bring out its truth? I believe so. The quote can be divided into three sub-claims. First, within metaphysical modality one finds both fundamental *de re* and fundamental *de dicto* necessities. Second, one *may* find fundamental *de dicto* necessities outside metaphysical modality. And third, one will not find fundamental *de re* necessities outside metaphysical modality.

We know from Section 2.5 that Fine settles for a three-tier account of fundamental modalities: normative, natural (nomic), and metaphysical. As we did there, I shall leave aside the normative one (for now) and focus on the *alethic* modalities: the nomic and the metaphysical. I take the three sub-claims in turn.

First, we know that metaphysical modality originates for Fine (and as per our working conception since Section 2.4.2) in the essences of *things*. Some of these things are *particular* individuals, and thus their essences will generate *de re* necessities which, in flowing directly from the things' essential properties, will be fundamentally metaphysical. Socrates being essentially human, for instance, results in the fundamental *de re* necessity of *him being necessarily human*. Similarly, *all* humans being essentially humans generates the *de re* (and also fundamental) modal principle that all humans are necessarily human (in symbols, so that one can check this claim against Roy's quotation above, $\forall x(Hx \supset \Box Hx)$). But equally, some of these things are *properties*, and (NKE) – Natural Kind Essentialism, to recall Section 2.4.2 – is a rich source of examples here: for instance, *necessarily, all cats are mammals* (which differs from all cats are necessarily mammals); in symbols, $\Box \forall x(Cx \supset Mx)$, where 'C' and 'M' stand, respectively, for *being a cat* and *being a mammal*. The examples afforded by (NKE), let me remark, will be *de dicto* necessities *irrespective* of their (epistemic) status as analytic or synthetic. Explicit definitions are another rich source of examples (see Hale (2013, Sect. 11.2)): for instance, *necessarily, all squares have four straight sides*. In this case, the resulting *de dicto* necessities will be analytic. Whether analytic or synthetic, these *de dicto* modalities are also (much like the *de re* ones) fundamentally metaphysical: they follow directly (and solely) from essential properties. This concludes the reasons for the first sub-claim.

Second, the fact that the natural laws are all generalisations with no mention of particular individuals makes their necessity *de dicto*. Of Fine's quote, we can now understand what is meant by 'some forms of *de dicto* necessity may not be [fundamentally metaphysical]'. Indeed, there may be some *fundamental* nomic *de dicto* necessities; there will be some so long as some natural laws are metaphysically contingent. For, if there are, their nomic necessity does not, by the nature of the case, originate in essences.[47]

Lastly, the case for the third sub-claim is basically the point made in Section 2.5 against it being *nomically* necessary that Socrates is human. The laws of nature don't prescribe Socrates' humanity, as they don't prescribe any property of any object. Roy makes essentially the same point here:

> Insofar as the principles are necessary *de dicto*, they have nothing to do with the properties of particular individuals. So it does not follow from the principles that '$\Box\neg Rq$'. So, on the suggested account, '$\Diamond Rq$'. Maybe we get that necessarily no person is a rock – that there is no world where something is both a person and a rock. But it does not follow that a thing that is a person in one world, is not a rock in another. (Roy 2000, 61)

The context of Roy's quote is *metaphysical* modality, but the point is exactly the same: one does not get *de re* necessities (or impossibilities) from only *de dicto* necessities. (The reader will recall that, back in Section 2.4.2, this point made us include particular propositions in the set of *metaphysical axioms*; because, in the metaphysical case, embracing the possibility that Socrates (or any other entity, for that matter) could be anything was an option to rule out.) Indeed, a modality that is constrained exclusively by *de dicto* necessities will be very liberal when it comes to *de re* possibilities.

We now have a better understanding of the opening quote in this section (as well as of the full passage quoted in Section 2.5). Also, I intend the above as sufficient reasons for the claim that, as far as *alethic* modalities are concerned, *fundamental, de re* necessities are to be found only within the metaphysical.

I did leave aside the normative modality, though. To wrap up this section, let me say in relation to this that, if normative modality is also, like the nomic one, constrained by generalisations, the same results apply to it, too. Moral particularists, however, might complain here, and this would need to be scrutinised (something I leave to the reader). For current purposes, that the case holds *at least* with the (limited) generality I have achieved – concerning alethic modalities – is sufficient.

3 Metaphysical Modality: Its Metaphysics

We're now leaving behind the topic of the varieties of modalities (and their relations to one another) to focus, more deeply than we did above, on

---

[47] See Fine's (2005, Sect. 2) own ingenious argument for the existence of such necessities. The argument, in conceding *scientific essentialism* – a view which implies that different natural laws will co-vary with different natural properties – is a particularly strong one.

metaphysical modality. Until recently, it wasn't uncommon to characterise metaphysical modality as *the absolute modality* among the alethic ones: that modality such that (i) its necessity is the least restrictive and (ii) its possibility, the most inclusive. And yet, various senses of *absoluteness*, not obviously equivalent (if equivalent at all), could accommodate (i) and (ii), proving this notion too obscure to be used as a first approximation to *metaphysical modality*. For instance, in Section 2.4.2 we characterised metaphysical modality as a type of modality intimately related to essentialism. The absoluteness of metaphysical modality thus understood derives (as seen in Section 2.5) from considering metaphysical necessity as that which is true in virtue of the nature of (*absolutely*) *all* things, without restriction. However, in a different sense, Lewis' target modality, which we referred to above as *combinatorial* modality, also has a claim to being *absolute*. For the limits of combinatorial modality (it can be argued) are provided by logic. As a result (with certain provisos in place, ruling out the truth of contradictions), combinatorial possibility is maximally inclusive: there's no sense of possibility, x, in which something p is x-possible without being *also* combinatorially possible.

Now, one might suggest that these two modalities are equivalent and, if this is so, it shouldn't be problematic that *it* comes out as absolute in those two senses. But, first, it is highly controversial that they are equivalent.[48] And second, regardless, the important remark for current purposes is that the senses of *absoluteness* on the basis of which metaphysical and combinatorial modalities can be said to be absolute are, although related, not quite the same. This sense disparity suffices to evidence the lack of clarity about what *absoluteness* amounts to.[49] As a notion with which to introduce (even illuminate) metaphysical modality, it is thus ill-suited.

Clarke-Doane (2021, Sect. 1861) goes even further than this: 'assuming that the [absoluteness] thesis is not merely terminological, and lacking in any metaphysical interest, it is an article of faith'. Without needing to go as far as Clark-Doane on this, I shall agree that it is best not to appeal to *absoluteness* to provide a first introduction to metaphysical modality.

Rather than having *absoluteness* as the axis of this section, therefore, I shall focus instead on the (also) much-contested question about *the source* of metaphysical modality. The target question is this: in virtue of what (if anything) are

---

[48] We know (as per Sections 2.4.2 and 2.5) that it is common to understand metaphysical modality as a *de re* modality (even as the only fundamentally *de re* modality), and we're about to see (Section 3.1) that combinatorial modality is a *de dicto first* modality that, without supplementation from counterpart theory, is arguably even *undefined* for singular propositions.

[49] See Hale (2012) for more on this unclarity. And for ways to legitimise talk of absolute modality, see Mallozzi (in press).

metaphysical modal claims true? And I shall address also several further questions in its vicinity. From where does metaphysical modality emerge? Is modality fundamental, or can it be reduced to something non-modal? Is metaphysical modality real, and, if it is, is it a mind-independent phenomenon? We will explore some rival answers to these questions – which we have had a scattered taste of in the previous section. My own theoretical preferences will become apparent, but the main aim of the section is not to argue for any of the answers but, rather, to make us appreciate the landscape of options. Inevitably, we don't have space to consider all the views, but the selection below is representative enough.

3.1 Lewisian Concretism

Lewisian Concretism is arguably the reductive view of modality par excellence.[50] As seen in Section 2.7, Lewis analyses his target modality (which we called *combinatorial*) in terms of possible worlds. To recall, for all purely general propositions, p:

$\Box p$ is true if and only if p is true *in* all possible worlds.
$\Diamond p$ is true if and only if p is true *in* some possible world.

This analysis is not merely intended as an extensional one but also as a definitional one: what it *means* for one such p to be possible is that there is a world where p; and what it *means* for one such p to be necessary is that p is true at all the worlds there are. For instance, what it means for the (purely general) proposition that *there are talking donkeys* to be possible is for there to be a possible world *where there are* talking donkeys.

Jennifer Wang (2015) has conveniently introduced a distinction that will help us classify the different accounts of modality to be seen in this section. This is the distinction between *de re first* and *de dicto first* accounts: 'the former ground all modal facts in *de re* modality, the latter in *de dicto* modality' (Wang 2020, 189). And we can agree with Wang that Lewis' account is a *de dicto first* account:

> The biconditional straightforwardly holds for *de dicto* modal claims – but Lewis also needs a way to make sense of *de re* modal claims, since individuals are worldbound on his view. His solution is counterpart theory. According to counterpart theory, a *de re* modal claim like 'I could have had a sister' [is] true in virtue of my having a counterpart in some world that has a sister. This counterpart is relevantly similar to me, where what counts as

---

[50] See Baldwin (2002) for doubts about it and Cameron (2012) for a thorough discussion of various other objections against the reductive power of Lewisian concretism.

relevantly similar is supplied by context. *De re* modality is thus reduced to *de dicto* modality on Lewis's view. (Wang 2020, 190)

For many contemporary modal metaphysicians, it would be combinatorial modality, *once supplemented* with counterpart theory, that has a serious claim to be identified as metaphysical modality. Thus supplemented, the analysis turns into the following: for any proposition *p*, purely general *or otherwise*:

□p is true if and only if p is true *according to* all possible worls,[51]
◊p is true if and only if p is true *according to* some possible world,

where the counterpart relation increases the representational power of the plurality of worlds: the world where Wang's counterpart has a sister is one *according to which* Wang (herself) has a sister.

This being so, metaphysical modality so understood still *reduces* to truth at/ according-to worlds, and this reducibility renders metaphysical modality non-fundamental: the source of metaphysical modality is *plain truth*, namely, truth at (or according to) worlds. To the extent that such reduction is not seen as a deflation (and it arguably should not be seen as such), Lewisian Concretism is a realist approach and, quite straightforwardly, therefore, a mind-independent one: what worlds there are is a mind-independent matter and, consequently, so is what is possible and what is necessary.

Lewisian Concretism has been highly discussed and, as anticipated in Section 2.7, it isn't a popular view among modal metaphysicians.[52] However, I urge the reader to familiarise themselves with Wilson's *quantum modal realism* for a Lewisian account that (pending scrutiny) is admirably well placed, at least in principle, to allay some of the strongest reasons to be reluctant about Lewis' account. Notwithstanding this, in contemporary literature the prevalent trend of thought, on which I have relied (in Section 2.4.2) in order to introduce the notion of *metaphysical modality*, is to analyse (and define) it in terms of essence.

3.2 Essentialist Theories

Essentialist Views of metaphysical modality constitute a vast family and space doesn't allow me to present them individually. And even when presenting them jointly, I shall do so in broad strokes, unavoidably not doing adequate justice to

---

[51] Or more aptly, for reasons we can't go into, '□p is true if and only if p is false *according to* no possible world'. See Lewis (1986, Sect. 4.4).

[52] The view has been extensively discussed and criticised from several quarters. Some objections have already been considered in Lewis (1986, Ch. 2). For a sample discussion, see Divers (1999), Divers and Fletcher (2020), Divers and Melia (2002), Divers and Parry (2017), Kripke (1972/ 1980), Lycan (1991), Parsons (2007), Roca-Royes (2020), and Shalkowski and Bueno (2000).

them. With this cautionary remark in place, the most salient common trait of these accounts is, in Hale's words, the idea that 'metaphysical necessities have their source in the natures [essences] of things, and [that] metaphysical possibilities are those left open by the natures of things' (Hale 2013, 253). In Wang's terms, again, Essentialist Views of metaphysical modality are undoubtedly *de re first*, quite in line with Fine's conception (as seen in Sections 2.5 and 2.8) that metaphysical modality is the only one to be fundamentally *de re*. It is precisely Fine's (1994) 'Essence and Modality' that inaugurated this contemporary – broadly neo-Aristotelian – family of views. Here, Fine argues for a *definitional* account of essence: essences are *real* definitions, that is, definitions of things (as opposed to definitions of the *nominal* type, which are of words).

This real-definition account of essence stands in opposition to the up-to-then traditional *modal account* of essence, which analyses them, reductively, in modal terms. Crudely, according to the modal account of essence, for a property to be essential to a given object is for it to be a necessary property of that object. If one reduces essence to modality, one cannot in turn (on pain of vicious circularity) identify essences as the source of modality. Thus, it is precisely because of its departure from the modal account, that Finean Essentialism, as we might call it, opens the door to accounts that ground modality in essence. And this is a theoretical opportunity that has been taken up, as indicated above, by a vast family of philosophers, which include Correia and Skiles (2019, 2021), Hale (2002, 2013, 2018), Kment (2006b, 2014), Lowe (2008, 2012), Peacocke (1999, 2002), and Tahko (2017, 2018), and others.[53]

Because they ground modality in essences, *structurally*, the mind-independence (or else mind-dependence) of modality will, on these accounts, be inherited by their proponents' views on the mind-independence (or else mind-dependence) of essence, and there is theoretical room to go either way. Typically, however, such theorists share a broadly neo-Aristotelian framework, and thus they tend to agree in viewing the phenomena as mind-independent. More disagreement is to be found, however, about the extent of the reduction of modality to essence. On this, Vaidya and Wallner ask the following:

> [Is] the notion of 'essence', which modality is grounded in, itself a modal notion? With regard to the two possible answers to this question, we can distinguish two positions, Reductive Finean Essentialism (RFE) and Non-Reductive Finean Essentialism (NRFE); both of which endorse (FE), i.e. that modality is grounded in essences.

---

[53] To extend the list a little, the following are philosophers whose modal views are shaped too, though to varying degrees, by Finean Essentialism: Godman, Mallozzi, and Papineau (2020), Jago (2021), Rosen (2015), Wallner (2020), Wallner and Vaidya (2020), and Williamson (2007, 2013).

(RFE) Essences are entirely non-modal.
(NRFE) Essences are in some sense modal. They belong to the larger family of modality. (Vaidya and Wallner 2021, Sect. 1927)

There has been a tendency to take Finean Essentialism to provide a reductive account of modality, whereby modality is reduced to essence, and essence becomes a primitive. But Penelope Mackie, for instance, has argued against 'the viability of an account of essence in terms of real definition that is both non-modal and yet yields the result that essential properties are also necessary properties' (Mackie 2020, 262). In this spirit, some authors conscientiously distance themselves from reductivism. Hale (2013, 150 fn. 12), for instance, thinks that 'a major difference between my theory and Fine's [is that while] Fine sees himself as giving a reductive explanation of modality in terms of essence or nature, I do not. This means that the two theories incur quite different explanatory obligations.'

Hale puts forward a non-reductive essentialist theory of modality, whereby essences are themselves modal. On his account, we can explain metaphysical modality *in general* by appeal to essences, thus succeeding in identifying the source of modality. This is so because, despite the fact that essences are modal – they are themselves necessary and thus have *unexplained* modal import – the explanations of modality in terms of essence are *non-transmissive*, which, in the current context, is to be understood as explanations 'of the form '$\Box$p because q' in which the *explanans*, q, is indeed necessary ... but in which what explains the necessity of the *explanandum* is not q's *necessity*, but its *truth simpliciter*' (Hale 2013, 131).

To appreciate Hale's point, note that such non-transmissive explanations would be equally available (at least in principle) to someone who held essential facts to be contingent.[54] It would still be available to such a philosopher to explain $\Box$p in terms of essence (simpliciter), compatibly with holding essences to be contingent (resulting in some of those necessities being themselves contingent: $\neg\Box\Box$p). More recently, and in a similar way to Hale, Wilsch (2017) has put forward Sophisticated Modal Primitivism, a view that, in the terms of the current discussion, is also to be received as a form of non-reductive essentialism. The key move of Wilsch's view is to characterise essences as *essentially* modal, thereby making them good candidates as the sources of metaphysical modality: their being essentially modal amounts to them encoding principles to the effect that the essential feature they are about is necessary of the object.

---

[54] Famously like Salmon (1981), as noted in Lewis (1986, 244–6) or Peacocke (1999, 195–6) and scrutinised in Roca-Royes (2006, 2016) and Leslie (2011).

Despite the substantial differences among them, we can bring Essentialist Views of metaphysical modality together under the slogan 'essence is the mother of *metaphysical* necessity'. This slogan carries a commitment to a specific type of explanatory and ontological priority: essence is prior to metaphysical modality. But this feature has generated a lot of hostile literature. Some authors accuse these views of explanatory *incompleteness*. According to this line of objection, essence cannot be the sole mother of metaphysical necessity because it is incapable of explaining *all* the necessities that there (intuitively) are, thus leaving theoretically open more possibilities than, intuitively, the view should do, resulting in extensional inadequacy. What, for instance, is the source of the *necessity* of essences (for the non-reductive essentialist)? To the extent that these intuitive necessities are left unexplained, should the proponents of the view renounce them?

Others attack the explanatory *adequacy* of the theories. Quite often, this complaint traces back to a dissatisfaction with Fine's departure from the modal account of essence, which, in turn, results in closing down the theoretical option that Finean Essentialism opened: namely, that of grounding modality in essence at all.[55] A related but different challenge for essentialist theories of modality is that of accounting for the modal facts of *mere possibilia*; that is, entities that could but do not exist. Peacocke (2002) has taken up this challenge very seriously, in a way that makes it manifest that it might be a requirement for any essentialist view of modality that aspires to extensional and explanatory adequacy to work not just with *essences* (and essential properties) but also with *individual essences* (and sufficiency properties). On this particular challenge, the *necessitists* among the essentialists are an exception:[56] their specific way of denying the existence of *mere possibilia* allows them to accommodate intuitions about 'them' while securing extensional adequacy. The problem for them, on the other side of the coin, is one of ontological commitment and believability: for them, a possible child of Wittgenstein *exists*, and is *non-concrete* yet *essentially human*.[57]

3.3 Dispositionalism

In this context, it is most pertinent to turn to Barbara Vetter's Potentialism, a type of Dispositionalism in modality which is undoubtedly also a *de re first*

---

[55] For examples of the former, see Cameron (2008) and Whittle (2010). For examples of the latter, see Casullo (2020), Leech (2021), Mackie (2020), Noonan (2018), Romero (2019) and Wildman (2021). See also Correia (2012) for a suggested refinement of the very pillar of Finean Essentialism.

[56] See those referred to in footnote 10.

[57] I have presented these problems at greater length in Roca-Royes (2011b).

account of metaphysical modality. There are other thorough dispositionalist theories of modality,[58] but what makes Vetter's especially salient for our purposes is not just the positive view per se, developed in Vetter (2015) and refined in Vetter (2021), but also the comparative criticism against the Essentialist Views contained in the latter piece.

Given that a core difference between Essentialism and Dispositionalism is a structural one, we can start by identifying it from the outset to then flesh out, albeit briefly, Vetter's Dispositionalism. The main difference is one of explanatory priority, and this difference is better appreciated having identified some shared standpoints. First, as noted in Section 3.2, a *typical* Finean essentialist will be realist, and mind-independentist, about modality, and so will a dispositionalist. Also, both types of views account for modality in a *de re first* manner or, as Vetter aptly calls it, in a 'localized manner': the essentialist localises the source of modality in the essences of *things*, and, the potentialist, in *their* potentialities.[59] Against this background of similarities, the differences are, sharply, as follows:

> *Essentialism* gives a direct account only of necessity: it is necessary that *p* just in case it is true in virtue of the essence of all objects taken together that *p* . . . . Possibilities, on this view, do not require a positive account: the possible is simply that which is not necessarily not the case. Possibility marks that which is left open, which is not settled by the essences of things. [. . .]
>
> *Potentialism*, on the contrary, gives a direct account only of possibility: it is possible that *p* just in case there are some objects *X* which have, had or will have an iterated potentiality for *p*, where an iterated potentiality is, roughly, a potentiality for further potentialities. . . . Necessities, on this view, do not require a positive account: the necessary is simply that which is not possibly not the case. Necessity marks the boundaries of potentiality; it arises where potentialities give out. (Vetter 2021, 834)

With the key difference identified, let us see how Vetter's potentialist story gets fleshed out. For Vetter, modality is grounded in potentialities. The conception of a *potentiality* is a theoretical generalisation from that of a *disposition*. Vetter (2015, Ch. 3) offers the core of her positive account of dispositions, which, as

---

[58] See Borghini and Williams (2008) and Jacobs (2010).

[59] Vetter also identifies *actualism* as a trait of Finean essentialism (Vetter 2021). And she is right that, in intent, they might all be so. But Peacocke's views constitute a counterexample to the claim. See especially Peacocke (2002), where he develops a *possibilist* essentialist account of *possibilia* to supplement his theory of modality. So, arguably, does Lowe (e.g., Lowe 2008, 2012), view in taking essence to precede existence, and possibility to precede actuality (as argued in Tahko 2022). Admittedly, the ontological commitments of some of these possibilisms might be light enough for the resulting theories to still count as actualists, despite the labels; this might especially be so of Peacocke's *propositional* possibilism.

she tells us, is a *possibility conception* of dispositions, thus distancing herself from the standard, *conditional* conception. On her account, a disposition (e.g., *fragility*) is a potentiality (e.g., *the potentiality to break*); but it is not always the case that a potentiality is a disposition (e.g., things don't need to be fragile for them to have the potentiality to break). For potentialities come in degrees and, whenever a given object, *x*, has the potentiality to φ – understood as *x can* φ – we speak of *x* having (also) the disposition to φ *only if* it can *easily* φ – that is, only if the degree of its potentiality is above a certain threshold, usually determined by context. Thus, starting out from the notion of a disposition, Vetter reaches that of a potentiality, where '[p]otentiality can now be recognized as the common genus of dispositions and such related properties as abilities' (Vetter 2015, 102). Because of the modal nature of potentialities, it's not an item in Vetter's agenda to reduce the modal to the non-modal: 'The account of possibility that I am offering is reductive in that it provides a straightforward definition of the possibility operator. It is not reductive in the sense of "reducing the modal to the non-modal". The notion of potentiality is a modal one if anything is' (Vetter 2015, 198).

Now, in line with the view's localised account of modality, potentialities reside in the things. A potentiality is always a potentiality for some object to do something, or to undergo something, etc. As a result, Vetter tells us, this doesn't fit the grammar of possibilities, which aren't so localised. To get a potentiality-based definition of possibility, we need to abstract the object away, and this is what Vetter does, thus putting forward this definition:

> POSSIBILITY It is possible that p=df Something has an iterated potentiality for it to be the case that p. (Vetter 2015, 197)

In connection with Section 2.8 (on the *de dicto/de re* distinction), note that *p* here can in principle be either purely general or else involve particular individuals. If the former (e.g., *pigs can run faster than humans*), however, the general possibility will be so *because* there are individuals that host the relevant potentialities (e.g., actual pigs hosting the potentiality to run faster than actual humans).

We must understand what the occurrence of 'iterated' means in this definition (as well as in the first quote above). To answer this, we should note that a preliminary question arises about the extensional adequacy of the account: are our worldly potentialities rich enough to deliver all the possibilities we intuitively think there are? What about the possibility that a granddaughter of mine lands on Mars? What about the possibility that the solar system disappears? Which object is the *bearer* of the corresponding potentialities? We won't be going into detail here, but extensional adequacy is certainly something that Vetter takes conscientious care of (like Finean essentialists). To do so, the theory incorporates a battery of different types of potentialities (extrinsic, joint, and iterated) that, together and in interaction with one another, allow Vetter to make at least a prima facie case for the extensional adequacy of her account (see especially Vetter (2015, Ch. 7)). And it is in this context that the notion of an *iterated* potentiality is vital. An iterated potentiality is, roughly, the potentiality for something to have further potentialities, of whichever type: simple, extrinsic, joint, or (already) iterated. By availing herself of iterated potentialities, Vetter greatly diminishes the risk of running out of potentialities before having accounted for all (intuitive) possibilities, something which would jeopardise the account's extensional adequacy.

Despite this prima facie case, Leech (2017) has put forward an insightful concern that strikingly mimics that of *mere possibilia* for the essentialists (flagged in Section 3.2). According to Leech, Vetter's account will, by design, struggle to account for many *de re* possibilities. She starts her complaint by calling attention to the (intuitive) possibility that a given object, *x*, might never have existed, and argues that, on Vetter's account, the corresponding potentiality should be hosted in *x*'s past by some *other* individual. Leech then further argues that there's nowhere in *x*'s past where that potentiality is to be found. After making her case about the possible non-existence of actual individuals, Leech explains why

> the problem quickly escalates. Any potentiality concerning a future but not yet present object will be affected. . . . There is, then, a general problem to account for *de re* possibilities for how things might have been otherwise. In any case where we need to look to the past to ground a possibility for an individual – before that individual existed – we cannot guarantee a possibility for that particular individual. (Leech 2017, 464)

Another criticism is offered by Wang (2020). She argues that Vetter's Potentialism cannot adequately account for *de dicto* modality. For instance, for any given negatively charged entity, *x*, Potentialism is well equipped to account for *x*'s impossibility of being positively charged. Vetter can do so by means of the notion of a *maximal potentiality*: a potentiality that must manifest. Taking *x*'s potentiality to be negatively charged to be a maximal disposition, we get that *x* must be negatively charged, thus yielding that it cannot be positively charged. Generalising from here (*x* is arbitrary after all), we get that *no* negatively charged object can be positively charged. Wang rightly notes, however, that this generalisation is still a *de re* modal claim, one that attributes to all existing negatively charged objects the impossibility of being positively charged. As such, it falls short of the target *de dicto* claim, 'Necessarily, no negatively charged objects are positively charged.' If this is on the right track, there is more to be developed to accommodate such *de dicto* claims – if they must be – under Vetter's Potentialism.

I leave it to the reader to decide whether one should be persuaded by Wang's concern. In connection with things that have been developed in earlier sections of this Element (for instance Section 2.8), however, I shall wrap this concern up with a note and a suggestion. The note is that the Essentialist Views, in taking it that properties (and not just particulars) have essences, would easily be able to explain the *de dicto* necessities that Wang raises concerns about. The target *de dicto* necessity above, for instance, would have its source in the 'incompatibility relation between the property of being negatively charged and the property of being positively charged' (Wang 2020, 193). In view of this, the potentialist might want to take up Wang's (2020, 196) suggestion and explore the idea that both particulars *and* properties host potentialities.

A related concern (and the last to be sketched here) that one could voice against Vetter's (or any other) Dispositionalism is about the kind of modality it delivers. Given that the view starts by focusing on *ordinary* dispositions and abilities, is Dispositionalism theorising about *metaphysical* modality, or is it theorising about a more mundane type of modality, for instance, a sort of *practical* or *circumstantial* modality? Maybe the account theorises about a family of them (and Vetter's use of the plural in speaking about circumstantial modalities suggests so), but is *metaphysical* modality ever among the type of modalities her potentialism delivers? The concern is that those modalities tend to be broader necessities than the metaphysical: maybe I can't jump across a given stream in most of the practical senses that will ever be relevant to me, but I can still jump it in the metaphysical sense.

This issue is dialectically relevant in that it might be thought to give the essentialist a distinctive advantage: we saw in Section 2.4.2 how essence is taken to imply *metaphysical* modality and, as such, there isn't scope for the analogous concern in the case of essentialists. The following remarks, however, should make it clear that the dispositionalist has all the ingredients needed to put this concern to rest. The main ingredient is the *locality* of modality inherent, as we saw above, to Dispositionalism (as well as to Essentialism). Whether in their essences or in their potentialities, the target modality, for the essentialists and the dispositionalists alike, *is born in things*. In Wang's terms, again, the accounts are of the *de re first* type. As such, the modality on Vetter's plate is primarily *de re*, and the necessities she gets (recall her notion of a *maximal potentiality*) will thus be fundamentally *de re*. At this point, one only needs to agree with Fine's claim that only *metaphysical* necessities (among the fundamental ones) are fundamentally *de re* in order to be content that the modality delivered by the dispositionalist is the intended, metaphysical one. (And we have seen reasons in Section 2.8 to agree with this claim.)

But haven't I just said that the various necessities Vetter starts theorising from are broader than the metaphysical one? At this point, recall also (from Section 2.5), that Fine suggests that, from metaphysical necessity, we can get narrower necessities by *restriction*, and that 'each of them can be regarded as a *species* of metaphysical necessity' (Fine 2005, 237). In a similar vein, one can get broader necessities by (*non-reductive?*) *relativisation* from metaphysical modality. With this in mind, one might say that Vetter's Dispositionalism gives *explanatory* priority to (some of) these broader necessities (this is something in need of scrutiny, but not for this occasion). This (the analogy goes) would not make them any less metaphysical than the metaphysical modality that Vetter encounters with maximal potentialities, not even (as should be clear) by the lights of a Finean essentialist.

3.4 Mind-Dependent Accounts

The accounts of metaphysical modality seen so far, whether reductivist or not, all share, broadly, the idea that modality is mind-independent in a very robust manner: according to these accounts, modal truth is not up to us, as thinkers, in any way. Coming to know a metaphysical modal truth (thus understood) is, on these accounts, a remarkable cognitive success: a sign that we are adequately cognitively equipped to *discover* mind-independent modal truths. For several authors, however, to class such cognitive successes as 'remarkable' is to understate the puzzle they give rise to: it would be a plain mystery if we were able to know *at all* metaphysical modality, construed mind-independently. Since our perceptual system is confined to being affected by what is actual, a posteriori modal knowledge would be puzzling. But a priori modal knowledge is puzzling too: how could human mental activity be so well aligned with extramental truth, which is not up to us?

This puzzlement has traditionally fostered a family of views on the metaphysics of modality which, to some extent, reconceive modal truth, and in a way that would make modal knowledge somewhat less mysterious. Despite being very different, these views are referred to in the literature by means of labels such as 'mind-dependent', 'non-cognitivist', 'lightweight realist', 'thinker-dependent', 'anti-realist', etc. None of these labels are however univocal, and we should be cautious when using them.

With this warning, I shall focus in this section on three types of views which, I believe, all have a claim to be seen as mind-dependent accounts of modal truth.

As we shall see, they are all, at least in principle, at an advantage when it comes to explaining our knowledge of (metaphysical) modal facts.

Our first type of view is Modal Fictionalism, especially of a non-timid type as characterised by Rosen. Non-timid Fictionalism

> aims to be *a theory of possibility*, that is, an account of the truth conditions for modal statements, and hence of the facts that make modal statements true (Rosen 1990, 354).

A modal fictionalist achieves this by providing a theory of modal truth which is parasitic on a chosen theory of possible worlds, in Rosen's case, Lewis'. Rather than endorsing the chosen possible-worlds analysis of modality, however, they consider it a fiction and provide instead the following, alternative analysis: For any modal proposition, □p or ◊p,

□p if and only if, according to [the chosen possible-worlds analysis], □p; and ◊p if and only if, according to [the chosen possible-worlds analysis], ◊p

whereby the prefix 'according to . . .' cancels any ontological commitment to possible worlds. It is this dependence on a *created fiction* which renders Fictionalism (of this full blooded, or non-timid, type) a thinker-dependent account, as the truth-conditions now depend on the existence of a theory, created by a theorist. Rosen's account also borrows Lewis' (brief) epistemological remarks on modal knowledge to the effect, roughly, that we know about modal facts by the use of imagination (Lewis 1986, Sect. 2.4). But whereas those remarks hardly put the epistemological puzzlement to rest in the case of Lewisian Realism – on the contrary, how would human imagination and mind-independent modal truth be so (conveniently) aligned? – they do pre-empt it in the case of Rosen's Fictionalism:

> when we engage in [such] imaginative experiments, *the least we discover is what is true according to [the chosen possible worlds analysis]*. But for the fictionalist, that is enough. The modal facts just are facts of this kind. Thus for the fictionalist there is no special mystery as to why we should trust our imaginations as a guide to the modal truth. (Rosen 1990, 340)

While these epistemological remarks are spot on, Rosen's Fictionalism suffers on the metaphysical side: that metaphysical modal truth consists in truth at a fiction is not plausible, and the merits of the account are not enough to outweigh its implausibility (see Nolan 2020, Sects. 3–4).

I turn now to the second and third types of view: Conventionalism and Quasi-Realism. We can group them together as a family of otherwise different views that nonetheless converge in taking the unimaginability of *not-p* to play (to varying degrees) a *constitutive* role in p's necessity. Consider for instance a view according to which what it means to say that a proposition p is impossible *just is* that we're unable to imagine p to be true. On this view, unimaginability plays a maximal constitutive role in metaphysical necessity (and impossibility). The relation however, while still constitutive, can be less close than that, as the following broad-strokes presentation of a classical triad helps to illustrate.

Classical thinker-dependent accounts that were developed in the 1980s include the *non-radical conventionalisms* of Craig (1985) and Wright (1980), and Blackburn's *non-conventionalist* Quasi-Realism (1986). According to the former, it is a matter of convention to regard certain claims as necessary (or possible or contingent). We won't go too much into this, but, briefly, the non-radicality of their views rests on the fact that, while the radical conventionalist would deny any possible axiomatisation of the class of necessary claims, according to the *non-radical* type there is a class of *conventional* necessities, C – whose negations we're unable to imagine – such that any other (conventionally) necessary claim can be said to be a consequence of some claim in C.[60] Blackburn's Quasi-Realism differs from them in that his account is emphatically *not* a conventionalist one. Blackburn would agree that *judging* that something is necessary consists in *realising* that one fails to be able to imagine its negation. On Wright's and Craig's views, however, realising that one cannot imagine ¬p is not enough for the judgement (hence truth) that *necessarily p*. It will be sufficient *only* under the appropriate kind of convention of doing so; hence the conventionalism of these accounts. In contrast, for Blackburn, there's no additional step to be taken: the modal is simply the vocabulary in which we express the imaginability states. For Blackburn, therefore, the constitutive role that imagination plays in modality is more intimate than in Craig's or Wright's views.

Within Conventionalism, Alan Sidelle's (1989) modal conventionalism offers an influential contemporary example.[61] The pre-Kripkean scene was largely conventionalist, with *analyticity* understood, by default, as the source of necessity and, *aprioricity*, its epistemic default.[62] Kripke's (1972/1980) a posteriori necessities, however, shook those defaults, generating a still-lasting wave of neo-Aristotelian

---

[60] The notion of *logical consequence* at play – the notion of what follows from what – may (Wright 1980) or may not (Craig 1985) *in turn* be a conventional matter; hence it is one of the main differences between the two accounts. But regardless, in both cases it would still be conventional that something *necessarily* follows from something else.

[61] See Sider (2011) for another contemporary conventionalist account, and Cameron (2021) for an introduction to conventionalism.

[62] See instances of this default in Ayer (1936/1952), Carnap (1947), and in Quine's arguments against metaphysical modality (Quine 1943, 1960).

essentialism (and *de re* modality) which brought with it a new mind-independence default for modality.[63] However, as indicated above, this carries with it the (presumed) disadvantage of epistemological puzzlement.

Sidelle's conventionalism developed as an explicit reaction to Kripkean a posteriori necessities. By conception, the theory thereby places a lot of emphasis on *distinctively* metaphysical necessities (and the essentialist thesis in their vicinity). Sidelle distinguishes between *real necessity* (roughly, what we're understanding here as mind-independent necessity) and *conventional necessity*, adding that '[r]eal necessity is something we would need to be forced into accepting' (Siddle 1989, 83). Against the received view, he then argues that the Kripkean a posteriori necessities don't have the required force to make us believe in real necessities. A paradigm example of such necessities is *necessarily, water is H_2O*. Kripke made a case that this necessity is synthetic and a posteriori. For Sidelle, however, there's a way of accommodating it back into conventionalism without neglecting it. Roughly, the strategy is to factor out this necessity into an a posteriori yet non-modal claim (namely, water is H_2O) and an *analytic* modal principle to the effect that *if water is H_2O then it is necessarily H_2O*: '[we] violate a convention by denying that it is necessary that water is H_2O while affirming that water is H_2O' (Sidelle 1989, 99).[64] The case generalises to other principles with traditional essentialist flavour, like the Necessity of Origins or the Necessity of Kind. In each case, Sidelle calls the corresponding analytic principle a *principle of individuation*; and they are, for him, the only source of alleged (*de re*) modality to be admitted. In sum, 'Modality does not find its home in the mind-independent world, but rather in us, in our ways of speaking and thinking, and thus the necessity is nothing beyond analyticity' (Sidelle 1989, 2).

While acknowledging that *analyticity* is a problematic phenomenon, Sidelle thinks that there are two major problems with real necessity which add up to a more serious problem than analyticity. One is the epistemological problem already cited – how could we possibly know of mind-independent modal facts?; the other, is metaphysical – what would mind-independent modal facts be, in the first place? (see, especially, Sidelle 1989, Ch. 4.) All in all, Sidelle thinks, we're far from being forced into *real modality*.

---

[63] Beyond Kripke (1972/1980) and also Putnam (1975a), see Matthews (1990) for an excellent portrait of the resurgent essentialist path leading up to Fine (1994).

[64] An analogous strategy is used by many contemporary modal *rationalists*, including those who, unlike Sidelle, hold modality to be a mind-independent phenomena (such as Hale (2013) and Peacocke (1999), among others). The same emphasis is not always placed on analyticity, though.

This sort of ontological and epistemological considerations that worry Sidelle and Rosen have long been identified as concerns that fuel mind-dependent accounts of modality, and we have witnessed this here with Fictionalism, Conventionalism, and Quasi-Realism. The next section is devoted to a view (the last to be seen in this Element) which, while sharing the ontological and epistemological motivations with those seen here, nonetheless resists being classed as mind-dependent.

3.5 Modal Normativism

In the words of Amie Thomasson, 'The ontological and epistemological difficulties encountered by both heavy-weight and Lewisian realist views of modality are enough to motivate developing a different understanding of modal discourse' (Thomasson 2007, 136).

Thomasson addresses these difficulties by denying that modal discourse has a descriptive function.[65] As we shall see in this section, modal truth comes out as mind-independent in her account, but not of a kind waiting to be discovered. Early expressions of non-descriptivism about modal discourse (especially Ayer's (1936/1952) and Wittgenstein's (1922/1933)) already had the ingredients to avoid those difficulties but, to Thomasson's puzzlement, they have been misunderstood and prematurely rejected, largely as a result of this misunderstanding. Her *modal normativism* is Thomasson's meticulous, contemporary contribution that aims to repair this historical oddity.

According to modal normativism, the function of *metaphysical* modal discourse is normative, rather than descriptive. That is, instead of being used to refer to (heavyweight) modal properties in the world, which would act as truth-makers for modal claims, modal vocabulary is claimed to be used to *mark*, within the object language – i.e., the language we use to speak about the world – certain rules. Typically, those rules are *expressible* in a meta-language – a language used to speak about a given object language. But, even when they are, and for reasons that Thomasson explains, it is useful to *also* have the resources to mark them in the object language (Thomasson 2013, 2020, Ch. 2).

The central tenet of modal normativism is thus that our (metaphysical) modal vocabulary serves those useful purposes, which explains why, according to the modal normativist, metaphysical modal vocabulary is not descriptive. 'On this view, which I have called "modal normativism", the basic function of talk about what's "metaphysically necessary" is not to try to describe modal features of the world, but rather to provide a particularly

---

[65] See Brandom (2008) for another contemporary non-descriptivist account.

useful way of expressing constitutive semantic and conceptual rules in the object language' (Thomasson 2013, 145).

For a stock example, consider 'Necessarily, all bachelors are men'. According to Thomasson, the term 'necessarily' in this modal statement *marks*, as that of *a rule*, the status of the indicative (and analytical) claim 'all bachelors are men'. In the meta-language, the rule can be expressed as something like 'do not apply "bachelor" to those to whom "men" doesn't apply'. That it is useful that we can mark this type of imperative in the object language stems from a variety of reasons. Among them, 'the indicative form of expression is far easier than the imperative to use in reasoning with rules, determining what follows from rules, and expressing conditional relations among rules' (Thomasson 2007, 138).

And, of the two types of indicatives that Thomasson distinguishes which would serve these facilitating purposes – namely, the simple indicative (as in *bachelors are men*) and the modal indicative (as in *necessarily, bachelors are men*) – the *modal* one has the added advantage of not being so easily mistaken for a description, plus that of allowing us to express permissions, too (Thomasson 2020, Ch. 2).

This normativist treatment can also be extended to claims of *ontological dependence*, 'traditionally stated in the form: Necessarily, if A exists, B exists' (Thomasson 2007, 143). These claims, as Thomasson acknowledges, are central in metaphysical discussions and it's thus important, for the salience of modal normativism, that they can also be subsumed under the same strategy: as marking certain rules of our language. 'These rules may take many different forms and may be much more complex than the simple rule "Apply 'bachelor' only where 'man' is applied", but the pattern is nonetheless the same' (Thomasson 2007, 144).

Does all this mean that, according to the modal normativist, (metaphysical) modal vocabulary is devoid of meaning? Being in a position to answer this question in the negative is very important for Thomasson. We won't go into the details here, but she offers, by way of a negative answer, introduction and elimination rules for modal vocabulary that she takes to be *meaning-constitutive* (Thomasson 2020, 83–4). These rules thus guarantee that modal statements (and modal discourse in general) are *truth-apt*, thus pre-empting concerns from this quarter, such as the Frege–Geach problem.[66] But not only this. As a modal normativist and an easy ontologist (Thomasson 2015), she

---

[66] See Schroeder (2008) for insightful discussion on this problem. Although this article is focused on the problem as it arises in metaethics, the problem for Thomasson's modal normativism would be structurally analogous if she was not in a position to provide truth-conditions for modal claims.

can agree with the heavyweight modal realist *that there are* modal properties and modal facts. Their disagreement is not about the truth-value of this existential claim, but rather one of direction of explanation. While for the heavyweight mind-independent theorist these modal facts and properties are, *antecedently*, the truth-makers of modal claims, and thus what explains modal truth, for the modal normativist modal truth (once guaranteed by the meaningfulness of the modal vocabulary) explains our talk of modal properties and facts: as sheer 'hypostatizations out of modal truths' (Thomasson 2009, 18).

In the remainder of this section, I shall focus on two other potential concerns that soon come to mind about this metaphysics of modality: the first is about Kripkean a posteriori necessities; and the second is about how modal normativism about *metaphysical* modality interacts with other kinds of alethic modalities.

As mentioned in Section 3.4 when considering modal conventionalism, Kripkean (*de re*) a posteriori necessities fuelled the idea that metaphysical modality wasn't to be seen as born of analyticity. In Thomasson's (2007, 144) terms, 'De re modal claims lend the most weight to heavyweight realist views, as they seem to describe objects as possessing genuine modal properties'. The way Thomasson accommodates them into her normativist programme is not distanced from the way we've seen Sidelle accommodates them into his conventionalism. For instance, Thomasson explains *the necessity of Hilary Clinton's genetic origins* in terms of a rule that allows us to co-apply the term 'Hilary Clinton' to x and y only when 'same person' applies to them, where, in turn, the rule governing 'same person' requires traceability back to the same genetic origins. Similarly, water's being necessarily H_2O can be accommodated by appealing to the schematic rule: 'Whatever the actual chemical composition of this stuff turns out to be, apply "water" only where there is stuff of that chemical structure', plus (empirical) contribution from the world about how to fill in the schematic slots (Thomasson 2007, 144–5; see also Thomasson 2020, Sect. 4.1). One might wonder, however, whether these strategies deliver a phenomenon of the appropriate strength (that is, the strength expected of metaphysical modality) as opposed to something weaker, more aptly referred to by 'always' than by 'necessarily', akin, for instance, to the fact that genetic origins are *perennial* properties and that water being H_2O is a *universal* truth. Here, I simply register this concern, without scrutinising it.[67]

---

[67] See Mallozzi (2023) for a discussion of what I take to be an expression of the same concern, or at least one in its vicinity. On behalf of the modal normativist one might reply that these perennial/universal truths can be counterfactually 'exported' to other worlds, thus guaranteeing their

For current purposes, I am more interested in the second type of concern. This has to do with how Thomasson views the relation between metaphysical modality and other types of *alethic* modality, including the natural one, as well as the bunch of modalities that, as seen in Section 2.5, the Finean essentialist can construct by restriction on the metaphysical modality. As anticipated at the end of Section 2.6, the concern will now take us back to the prospects of unifying different types of modalities (alethic and beyond).[68]

Thomasson is clear from the outset that her large-scope project is that of unifying the treatment of *alethic* modal vocabulary in terms of deontic modality. Yet, in developing the project, she quickly narrows down the focus to that of *metaphysical* modality: 'The hope is instead to provide a way of understanding *alethic* modality in terms of deontic modality; more specifically, to make sense of claims about *metaphysical* necessity by way of understanding the normative rules for using our terms' (Thomasson 2007, 136–7; my italics).

The opening quote in this section identified Thomasson's motivations for treating metaphysical modality in normativist terms; these are the same metaphysical and epistemological difficulties that fuelled mind-dependent accounts (Section 3.4). My concern here, crudely put, is that the force of those motivations isn't enough to allow Thomasson to achieve her wide-reaching ultimate aim.[69] Indeed, the strength of these concerns is at its highest when we assess them, as Thomasson does, against 'specifically *metaphysically* modal claims'; claims of necessity and possibility in the vicinity of essentialist claims (Thomasson 2021, Sect. 2082). It quickly diminishes, however, when one assesses them against ordinary modal claims. Let me explain.

With respect to the *metaphysical* difficulties – of providing an account of the source of metaphysical modality – Vetter's Potentialism (as well as other dispositionalist accounts), for instance, offers a metaphysics of *possibility* that has among its virtues its lack of scientific extravagance. Admittedly, as seen at the end of Section 3.3, her starting focus is *ordinary* dispositions and abilities, which might be thought to concern more restricted forms of alethic possibilities. But we have seen there too how this does not make these forms of possibility *not* metaphysical. Rather, the suggestion was that, in her

---

necessity; and they can be so exported *even* when the linguistic rules might have been different in those alternative situations. See Locke and Thomasson (2023) for a discussion on Mallozzi, and Thomasson (2009, 8–9) for how, according to her, this resource was already present, in conception, in early modal non-descriptivists, such as Ayer.

[68] This concern is related to the first critical question in Chrisman and Scharp (2022, 4–5).

[69] The same would apply to Sidelle's conventionalism, if he wanted to extend it to other types of alethic modalities too.

account, these restricted possibilities are (ontologically) continuous with metaphysical possibility, the ultimate focus of Vetter's theorising. This being so, Dispositionalism offers a contemporary illustration of how to diminish the puzzlement about the metaphysics of *metaphysical* modality: it shouldn't exceed the (minor?) puzzlement about abilities or dispositions.

Now, delving much into the *epistemology* of (metaphysical) modality is not among the aims of this Element, but I shall say enough nonetheless to motivate the current point that Thomasson's epistemological concerns don't warrant a *unified*, normativist treatment of alethic modalities. With respect to these concerns, we should note that, largely simultaneously with the emergence of dispositionalist accounts of modality, the literature in the epistemology of modality is experiencing what we might call 'a non-rationalist turn'. Thomasson seems to share (with many contributors) the idea that *potentialism* in the metaphysics of modality goes very well with *non-rationalism* in the epistemology of modality. And while seemingly granting explanatory merits to both camps, she nonetheless writes that

> [v]iews that take modal properties to be features of this world, which we can come to know through broadly empirical/scientific means, certainly have the potential to ease at least some of the problems of modal epistemology. . . . But dispositions and counterfactuals are the modal properties of interest to *science* more than to *metaphysics* – and are crucially different from the modal claims typically at issue in metaphysical and other strictly philosophical debates.
>
> It is much less clear that anything along the lines of an empirical account of modal knowledge can be of use for specifically *metaphysical* modal claims. . . . [Roca-Royes] argues directly that the empirical method she defends for coming to know certain *de re* unrealized possibilities for concrete entities does not extend to give us knowledge of whether essentialist claims . . . are true. (Thomasson, 2021, Sect, 2082)

What is important to note from this quote (for current purposes) is that, in view of the recent developments she mentions, Thomasson herself seems to be neither as metaphysically nor as epistemically puzzled about the *non-specifically metaphysical* modalities as she is about the *specifically metaphysical* one. At this point, one would need to do a bit of exegesis about how best to receive the specifically/non-specifically distinction on metaphysical modal claims, but the context of the quote makes it clear that the specifically metaphysical ones include claims central to philosophy, including essentialist claims and, admittedly, many of the ones that (according to Leech's worries, as seen in Section 3.2) Vetter's dispositionalism would struggle (metaphysically) to account for.

But even if we granted Leech's and Thomasson's points – i.e., that some metaphysical and epistemological difficulties remain – the fact stands that there are *restricted* (or else *relativised*) types of modalities that are, in view of current developments, neither metaphysically nor epistemologically (as) puzzling as the specifically metaphysical one. And, for the reasons given in Sections 2.5 and 2.8, these modalities are still to be seen as metaphysical, even if not *specifically* so (i.e., even if they are not the absolute one).

Now, there is an increasing number of scientifically friendly modal accounts that demystify *some* metaphysical modalities (both their metaphysics and their epistemology) while retaining heavyweight mind-independence. In view of this, a normativist treatment *of them* would be under-motivated. And if this is so, the following is an urgent question for Thomasson: shouldn't we aim for an account of the *specifically metaphysical* modal claims that treats them as continuous with those more mundane metaphysical modal claims?

At this point, Thomasson might agree that it would be difficult to treat them discontinuously. And she might, in response, remind us that her wide-scope project is to treat *all* alethic modalities (metaphysical or not; specifically so or not) under the model of *modal normativism*. Indeed, she at places considers, in a sharply Humean spirit that we should not overlook, the idea of treating *natural* necessities as normative ones too: 'While metaphysical modalities are reflections of constitutive semantic or conceptual rules, the natural correlate view would take the physical necessities expressed in scientific laws to reflect norms of reasoning on the basis of empirical evidence, or something along those lines' (Thomasson 2020, 121).

But in response, my concern is that the unification that results from this can be diagnosed, in view of recent developments, as an overreaction: unification in the wrong direction. Epistemically, Thomasson is right that some puzzlement remains.[70] And it's true that more needs to be done on the metaphysical front too. And yet, recent developments should make us treat this remaining puzzlement as what it is (or as I believe it to be): a *remainder* of the initial one, small enough, it might be claimed, not to call for a metaphysical re-conception of *alethic modalities* across the board.[71]

---

[70] Although see Roca-Royes (2018) for ways to ameliorate this: I advocate for an ambitious, yet non-uniform epistemology of modality, rather than settling for a non-ambitious, uniform one.

[71] One can find examples of recent developments that ground such optimism in the Fischer and Leon (2017). Also, Strohminger (2015) and (Vetter 2023) are very good examples.

The 'descriptivist assumption' that Thomasson (2020, Ch. 1) rightly claims to be present in much of the literature on modality is, I contend, a default we should be forced out of.[72] And in view of the fact that the metaphysical and epistemological difficulties aren't particularly forceful for the restricted (non-specifically metaphysical) modalities, we aren't forced out of this assumption in their case. In this respect, and although Williamson (2016, 462), might be right that 'Arguments for scepticism about metaphysical modality tend to generalize to other objective modalities, irrespective of the theorist's intentions', the present point is rather that, in Thomasson's case, the reasons for her normativism don't generalise, *despite* her intentions. To the extent that this is so, it would be by brute force that one could achieve wide-scope, *unified* normativism.

It is pertinent at this point to ask what are the alternative options. One option is to remain in the descriptivist default *across the board* and to learn to live with the remaining explanatory deficit (perhaps even acknowledging partial scepticism, as a reminder of our limitations). Another option is to endorse modal normativism only for the distinctively metaphysical modal claims, to the detriment of the unified treatment. Of these two, my preference is for the former. Developing this option is something I leave for a future occasion, and I wrap up this section merely stating what I consider to be its important advantage. Heavyweight realism about the metaphysical modalities (all of them) is best placed to explain what seems to me to be a fundamental difference between the metaphysical and the normative necessities, namely, that only the latter *can* (in a metaphysical sense) be transgressed: you must *change the game* to do the alethically impossible, but you *cheat in the game* if you do the normatively impossible. This difference (which, as seen in Section 2, turns on principle (M): $\Box p \rightarrow p$) is lost, one might fear, with a treatment of any metaphysical modality in terms of normative modality.

4 Concluding Remarks

At first sight, the focuses of Sections 2 and 3 are quite different: Section 2 was devoted to the varieties of modalities and their relations to one another, whereas Section 3 centred on (the metaphysics of) metaphysical modality. The discussion in this Element reveals, however, that these two areas of the discipline are largely entrenched with one another. Indeed, as observed, unification (or non-unification) agendas are not neutral on the *metaphysics* of the different types of modalities, the metaphysical included.

---

[72] In clear opposition to Sidelle (1989, 83) who (as seen in Section 3.4) considers it 'something we need to be forced into accepting'.

Despite the transpiration of theoretical preferences, nothing in the above is intended as conclusive. My primary aim has been, instead, dialectical: that of depicting some of the debates taking place in some of the most recent literature, and providing the reader with the resources to identify their own position in that landscape.

References

Armstrong, David M. (1989). *A Combinatorial Theory of Possibility*. Cambridge: Cambridge University Press.

Ayer, A. J. (1936/1952). *Language, Truth and Logic*. New York: Dover.

Baldwin, Tom. (2002). Kantian Modality. *Aristotelian Society Supplementary Volume*, 76(1): 1–24.

Berto, Franz. (2010). Impossible Worlds and Propositions: Against the Parity Thesis. *Philosophical Quarterly*, 60(240): 471–86.

Berto, Franz, and Jago, Mark. (2018). Impossible Worlds. In *The Stanford Encyclopedia of Philosophy*, edited by Edward N. Zalta, https://plato.stanford.edu/archives/fall2018/entries/impossible-worlds/.

Blackburn, Simon. (1986/1993). Morals and Modals. In *Essays in Quasi-Realism*. Oxford: Oxford University Press, 52–74.

Boghossian, Paul. (1996). Analyticity Reconsidered. *Noûs*, 30(3): 360–91.

Boghossian, Paul and Williamson, Timothy. (2020). *Debating the A Priori*. Oxford: Oxford University Press.

Borghini, Andrea. (2016). *A Critical Introduction to the Metaphysics of Modality*. London: Bloomsbury Publishing.

Borghini, Andrea and Williams, Neil. (2008). A Dispositional Theory of Possibility. *Dialectica*, 61(1): 21–41.

Brandom, Robert. (2008). *Between Saying and Doing: Towards an Analytic Pragmatism*. Oxford: Oxford University Press.

Brody, Baruch. (1967). Natural Kinds and Real Essences. *Journal of Philosophy*, 64: 431–46.

Bueno, Otavio and Shalkowski, Scott. (2009). Modalism and Logical Pluralism. *Mind*, 118: 295–321.

Bueno, Otavio and Shalkowski, Scott. (2015). Modalism and Theoretical Virtues: Toward an Epistemology of Modality. *Philosophical Studies*, 172: 671–89.

Cameron, Ross. (2008). Truthmakers and Modality. *Synthese*, 164(2): 261–80.

Cameron, Ross. (2012). Why Lewis's Analysis of Modality Succeeds in Its Reductive Ambitions. *Philosophers' Imprint*, 12(8): 1–21.

Cameron, Ross. (2021). Modal Conventionalism. In *The Routledge Handbook of Modality*, edited by Otavio Bueno and Scott Shalkowski. Oxford: Routledge, 136–45.

Carnap, Rudolf. (1947). *Meaning and Necessity: A Study in Semantics and Modal Logic*. Chicago, IL: University of Chicago Press.

Casullo, Albert. (2020). Essence and Explanation. *Metaphysics*, 2: 88–96.

Chalmers, David. (1996). *The Conscious Mind*. New York: Oxford University Press.

Chalmers, David. (2002). Does Conceivability Entail Possibility? In *Conceivability and Possibility*, edited by Tamar Szabó Gendler and John Hawthorne. Oxford: Clarendon Press, 145–200.

Chalmers, David. (2004). Epistemic Two-Dimensional Semantics. *Philosophical Studies*, 118(1/2): 153–226.

Chrisman, Matthew, and Scharp, Kevin. (2022). Book Review of *Norms and Necessity*, by Amie Thomasson. *Mind*, zab094, https://doi.org/10.1093/mind/fzab094.

Cieśluk, Andrzej. (2010). *De Re/De Dicto* Distinctions (Syntactic, Semantic and Pragmatic Interpretation). *Studies in Logic, Grammar and Rhetoric*, 22 (35): 81–94.

Clarke-Doane, Justin. (2021). Metaphysical and Absolute Possibility. *Synthese*, 198(8): S1861–72.

Correia, Fabrice. (2012). On the Reduction of Necessity to Essence. *Philosophy and Phenomenological Research*, LXXXIV(3): 639–53.

Correia, Fabrice, and Skiles, Alexander. (2019). Grounding, Essence, and Identity. *Philosophy and Phenomenological Research*, 98(3): 642–70.

Correia, Fabrice, and Skiles, Alexander. (2021). Modality, Essence, and Identity. *Mind*, fzab017, https://doi.org/10.1093/mind/fzab017.

Craig, Edward. (1985). Arithmetic and Fact. In *Exercises in Analysis*, edited by Ian Hacking. Cambridge: Cambridge University Press, 89–112.

Cresswell, Max, and Hughes, George. (1968). *An Introduction to Modal Logic*. Oxford: Methuen Young Books.

De, Michael. (2020). A Modal Account of Essence. *Metaphysics*, 3(1): 17–32.

DeRosset, Louis. (2009a). Possible Worlds I: Modal Realism. *Philosophy Compass*, 4(6): 998–1008.

DeRosset, Louis. (2009b). Possible Worlds II: Non-Reductive Theories of Possible Worlds. *Philosophy Compass*, 4(6): 1009–21.

Divers, John. (1999). A Genuine Realist Theory of Advanced Modalizing. *Mind*, 108(430): 217–39.

Divers, John. (2002). *Possible Worlds*. New York: Routledge.

Divers, John and Fletcher, Jade. (2020). (Once Again) Lewis on the Analysis of Modality. *Synthese*, 197(2): 4645–68.

Divers, John and Melia, Joseph (2002). The Analytic Limit of Genuine Modal Realism. *Mind*, 111(441): 15–36.

Divers, John and Parry, John. (2017). Advanced Modalizing *De Dicto* and *De Re*. *Analysis*, 78(3): 415–25.

Edgington, Dorothy. (2004). Two Kinds of Possibility. *Proceedings of the Aristotelian Society, Supplementary Volumes*, 78: 1–22.

Fine, Kit. (1994). Essence and Modality: The Second Philosophical Perspectives Lecture. *Philosophical Perspectives*, 8: 1–16.

Fine, Kit. (2005). The Varieties of Necessity. In *Modality and Tense*. Oxford: Oxford University Press, 235–60.

Fischer, Bob and Leon, Felipe (eds.). (2017). *Modal Epistemology after Rationalism*, Synthese Library 378. Cham: Springer International Publishing.

Forbes, Graeme. (1985). *The Metaphysics of Modality*. Oxford: Clarendon Press.

Forbes, Graeme. (1989). *Languages of Possibility: An Essay in Philosophical Logic*. Oxford: Basil Blackwell.

Forbes, Graeme. (2001). Origins and Identities. In *Individuals, Essence and Identity, Themes of Analytic Metaphysics*, edited by Andrea Bottani, Massimiliano Carrara, and Pierdaniele Giarretta. Dordrecht: Kluwer, 319–40.

Gallois André. (1998). *De Re, De Dicto*. In *Routledge Encyclopedia of Philosophy*, edited by Edward Craig, www.rep.routledge.com/articles/thematic/de-re-de-dicto/v-1.

Gendler, Tamar Szabó and Hawthorne, John (eds.). (2002). *Conceivability and Possibility*. Oxford: Clarendon Press.

Glazier, Martin. (2022). *Essence*, Elements in Metaphysics. Cambridge: Cambridge University Press.

Godman, Marion, Mallozzi, Antonella, and Papineau, David. (2020). Essential Properties Are Super-Explanatory: Taming Metaphysical Modality. *Journal of the American Philosophical Association*, 6(3): 316–34.

Hale, Bob. (2002). The Source of Necessity. *Philosophical Perspectives*, 16: 299–319.

Hale, Bob. (2012). What Is Absolute Necessity? *Philosophia Scienciate*, 16(2): 117–48.

Hale, Bob. (2013). *Necessary Beings: An Essay on Ontology, Modality, and the Relations between Them*. Oxford: Oxford University Press.

Hale, Bob. (2018). *Essence and Existence*, edited by Jessica Leech. Oxford: Oxford University Press.

Hale, Bob, and Leech, Jessica. (2017). Relative Necessity Reformulated. *Journal of Philosophical Logic*, 46(1): 1–26.

Humberstone, Lloyd. (1981). Relative Necessity Revisited. *Reports on Mathematical Logic*, 13: 33–42.

Jackson, Frank. (1998). *From Metaphysics to Ethics: A Defence of Conceptual Analysis*. Oxford: Oxford University Press.

Jacobs, Jonathan. (2010). A Powers Theory of Modality: Or, How I Learned to Stop Worrying and Reject Possible Worlds. *Philosophical Studies*, 151: 227–48.

Jago, Mark. (1996). Advanced Modalizing Problems. *Mind*, 125(499): 627–42.

Jago, Mark. (2021). Knowing How Things Might Have Been. *Synthese*, 198: 1981–99.

Jubien, Michael. (2009). *Possibility*. Oxford: Oxford University Press.

Kaplan, David. (1989). Demonstratives. In *Themes from Kaplan*, edited by Joseph Almog, John Perry, and Howard Wettstein. Oxford: Oxford University Press, 481–563.

Kiourti, Ira. (2010). *Real Impossible Worlds: the Bounds of Possibility*. Ph.D. Dissertation, University of St Andrews.

Kment, Boris. (2006a). Counterfactuals and Explanation. *Mind*, 115(458): 261–309.

Kment, Boris. (2006b). Counterfactuals and the Analysis of Necessity. *Philosophical Perspectives*, 20: 237–302.

Kment, Boris. (2014). *Modality and Explanatory Reasoning*, Oxford: Oxford University Press.

Kment, Boris. (2021). Varieties of Modality. *The Stanford Encyclopedia of Philosophy*, edited by Edward N. Zalta, https://plato.stanford.edu/archives/spr2021/entries/modality-varieties/.

Knobe, Joshua, Olum, Ken, and Vilekin, Alexander. (2006). Philosophical Implications of Inflationary Cosmology. *British Journal for the Philosophy of Science*, 57(1): 47–67.

Kripke, Saul. (1972/1980). *Naming and Necessity*, Cambridge, MA: Harvard University Press.

Lange, Marc. (2005). A Counterfactual Analysis of the Concepts of Logical Truth and Necessity. *Philosophical Studies*, 125: 277–303.

Leech, Jessica. (2016). The Varieties of (Relative) Modality. *Pacific Philosophical Quarterly*, 97(2): 158–80.

Leech, Jessica. (2017). Potentiality. *Analysis*, 77(2): 457–67.

Leech, Jessica. (2020). Relative Necessity Extended. *Journal of Applied Logics*, 7(6): 1177–98.

Leech, Jessica. (2021). From Essence to Necessity via Identity. *Mind*, 130(519): 887–908.

Leslie, Sarah-Jane. (2011). Essence, Plenitude, and Paradox. *Philosophical Perspectives*, 25: 277–96.

Lewis, David. (1973). *Counterfactuals*. Oxford: Blackwell Publishers.

Lewis, David. (1986). *On the Plurality of Worlds*. Oxford: Blackwell Press.

Linsky, Bernard, and Zalta, Edward. (1994). In Defense of the Simplest Quantified Modal Logic. *Philosophical Perspectives*, 8: 431–58.

Linsky, Bernard, and Zalta, Edward. (1996). In Defense of the Contingently Nonconcrete. *Philosophical Studies*, 84: 283–94.

Locke, Theodore, and Thomasson, Amie. (2023). Modal Knowledge and Modal Methodology. In *Epistemology of Modality and Philosophical Methodology*, edited by Dusko Prelević and Anand Vaidya. New York: Routledge, 284–301.

Lowe, Jonathan. (2008). Two Notions of Being: Entity and Essence. *Royal Institute of Philosophy Supplement*, 62: 23–48.

Lowe, Jonathan. (2012). What Is the Source of Our Knowledge of Modal Truths? *Mind*, 121(484): 919–50.

Lycan, William. (1991). Two – No, Three – Concepts of Possible Worlds. *Proceedings of the Aristotelian Society* (New Series), 91: 215–27.

Mackie, Penelope. (1994). Sortal Concepts and Essential Properties. *Philosophical Quarterly*, 44: 311–33.

Mackie, Penelope. (2006). *How Things Might Have Been: Individuals, Kinds, and Essential Properties*. Oxford: Oxford University Press.

Mackie, Penelope. (2020). Can Metaphysical Modality be Based on Essence? In *Metaphysics, Meaning, and Modality. Themes from Kit Fine*, edited by Mircea Dumitru. New York: Oxford University Press, 247–64.

Mallozzi, Antonella. (2021a). Putting Modal Metaphysics First. *Synthese*, 198(S8): S1937–56.

Mallozzi, Antonella. (2021b). Two Notions of Metaphysical Modality. *Synthese*, 198(S6): 1387–1408.

Mallozzi, Antonella. (2023). Semantic Rules, Modal Knowledge, and Analyticity. In *Epistemology of Modality and Philosophical Methodology*, edited by Dusko Prelević and Anand Vaidya. New York: Routledge, 265–83.

Mallozzi, Antonella. (in press). What Is Absolute Modality? Special Issue on Pluralism, Relativism and Skepticism. *Inquiry: An Interdisciplinary Journal of Philosophy*.

Matthews, Gareth. (1990). Aristotelian Essentialism. *Philosophy and Phenomenological Research*, 50: 251–62.

McGinn, Colin. (1976). On the Necessity of Origins. *Journal of Philosophy* 73 (5): 127–35.

Melia, Joseph. (2003). *Modality*. Chesham, UK: Acumen.

Miller, Richard. (1992). Genuine Modal Realism: Still the Only Non-Circular Game in Town. *Australasian Journal of Philosophy*, 71(2): 159–60.

Nelson, Michael. (2019). The *De Re/De Dicto* Distinction. Supplement to Propositional Attitude Reports. In *The Stanford Encyclopedia of Philosophy* (Spring 2022 Edition), edited by Edward N. Zalta, https://plato.stanford.edu/archives/spr2022/entries/prop-attitude-reports/.

Nolan, Daniel. (1997). Impossible Worlds: A Modest Approach. *Notre Dame Journal of Formal Logic*, 38(4): 535–72.

Nolan, Daniel. (2013). Impossible Worlds. *Philosophy Compass*, 8(4): 360–72.

Nolan, Daniel. (2020). Modal Fictionalism. In *The Stanford Encyclopedia of Philosophy* (Spring 2022 Edition), edited by Edward N. Zalta, https://plato.stanford.edu/archives/spr2022/entries/fictionalism-modal/.

Noonan, Harold. (2014). The Adequacy of Genuine Modal Realism. *Mind*, 123 (491): 851–60.

Noonan, Harold. (2018). The New Aristotelian Essentialists. *Metaphysica*, 19: 87–93.

Parsons, Josh. (2007). Against Advanced Modalizing. Unpublished manuscipt, www.academia.edu/1016958/Against_advanced_modalizing.

Peacocke, Christopher. (1999). *Being Known*. Oxford: Oxford University Press.

Peacocke, Christopher. (2002). Principles for Possibilia. *Noûs*, 36(3): 486–508.

Plantinga, Alvin. (1974). *The Nature of Necessity*. Oxford: Oxford University Press.

Prelević, Duško, and Anand Vaidya. (2023). *Epistemology of Modality and Philosophical Methodology*. New York: Routledge.

Prior, Arthur. (1957). *Time and Modality*. Oxford: Clarendon Press.

Putnam, Hilary. (1975a). The Meaning of 'Meaning'. *Minnesota Studies in the Philosophy of Science*, 7: 215–71; reprinted in (Putnam 1975b).

Putnam, Hilary. (1975b). *Mind, Language and Reality* (Philosophical Papers, Volume 2). Cambridge: Cambridge University Press.

Quine, Willard Van Orman. (1943). Notes on Existence and Necessity. *Journal of Philosophy*, 40: 113–27.

Quine, Willard Van Orman. (1960). *Word and Object*. Cambridge, MA:MIT Press.

Reinert, Janine. (2013). Ontological Omniscience in Lewisian Modal Realism. *Analysis* 74(4): 676–82.

Robertson, Teresa. (2000). Essentialism: Origin and Order. *Mind*, 108: 299–307.

Robertson, Teresa, and Atkins, Philip. (2020). Essential vs. Accidental Properties. In *The Stanford Encyclopedia of Philosophy*, edited by Edward N. Zalta, https://plato.stanford.edu/archives/win2020/entries/essential-accidental/.

Roca-Royes, Sònia. (2006). Peacocke's Principle-Based Account: 'Flexibility of Origins' Plus S4. *Erkenntnis* 65(3): 405–26.

Roca-Royes, Sònia. (2011a). Essential Properties and Individual Essences. *Philosophy Compass*, 6(1): 65–77.

Roca-Royes, Sònia. (2011b). Essentialism vis-à-vis *Possibilia*, Modal Logic, and Necessitism. *Philosophy Compass*, 6(1): 54–64.

Roca-Royes, Sònia. (2012). Essentialist Blindness Would Not Preclude Counterfactual Knowledge. *Philosophia Scientiae* (Special Issue on Modalities: Semantics and Epistemology), 16(2): 149–72.

Roca-Royes, Sònia. (2016). Rethinking Origin Essentialism (for Artefacts). In *Reality Making*, edited by Mark Jago. Oxford: Oxford University Press, 153–78.

Roca-Royes, Sònia. (2017). Similarity and Possibility: An Epistemology of *De Re* Possibility for Concrete Entities. In *Modal Epistemology after Rationalism*, edited by Bob Fischer and Felipe Leon. Cham: Springer International Publishing, 221–45.

Roca-Royes, Sònia. (2018). Rethinking the Epistemology of Modality for Abstracta. In *Being Necessary. Themes of Ontology and Modality from the Work of Bob Hale*, edited by Ivette Fred-Rivera and Jessica Leech. Oxford: Oxford University Press, 245–65.

Roca-Royes, Sònia. (2020). Genuine Modal Realism, the Humean Thesis and Advanced Modalizing. *Synthese*, 197: 4669–90.

Romero, Carlos. (2019). Modality Is Not Explainable by Essence. *Philosophical Quarterly*, 69(274): 121–41.

Rosen, Gideon. (1990). Modal Fictionalism. *Mind*, 99: 327–54.

Rosen, Gideon. (2015). Real Definition. *Analytic Philosophy*, 56(3): 189–209.

Roy, Tony. (2000). Things and *De Re* Modality. *Noûs*, 34(1): 56–84.

Russell, Gillian. (2008). *Truth in Virtue of Meaning: A Defence of the Analytic/ Synthetic Distinction*. Oxford: Oxford University Press.

Russell, Gillian. (2014). Metaphysical Analyticity and the Epistemology of Logic. *Philosophical Studies*, 171: 161–75.

Salmon, Nathan. (1981). *Reference and Essence*. Princeton, NJ: Princeton University Press.

Schroeder, Mark. (2008). What Is the Frege–Geach Problem? *Philosophy Compass*, 3(4): 703–20.

Sellars, Wilfrid. (1953). Inference and Meaning. *Mind*, 62(247): 313–38.

Shalkowski, Scott. and Bueno, Otavio. (2000). A Plea for a Modal Realist Epistemology. *Acta Analytica*, 15(24): 175–93.

Shoemaker, Sidney. (1980). Causality and Properties. In *Time and Cause*, edited by Peter van Inwagen. Dordrecht: D. Reidel Publishing Company, 109–36.

Shoemaker, Sidney. (1998). Causal and Metaphysical Necessity. *Pacific Philosophical Quarterly*, 79: 59–77.

Sidelle, Alan. (1989). *Necessity, Essence, and Individuation*, Ithaca, NY: Cornell University Press.

Sider, Theodor. (2002). The Ersatz Pluriverse. *Journal of Philosophy*, 99: 279–315.

Sider, Theodor. (2011). *Writing the Book of the World*. Oxford: Oxford University Press.

Smiley, Timothy. (1963). Relative Necessity. *Journal of Symbolic Logic*, 28(2): 113–34.

Soames, Scott. (2004). *Reference and Description. The Case against Two-Dimensionalism*. Princeton, NJ: Princeton University Press.

Stalnaker, Robert. (1976). Possible Worlds.*Noûs*, 10(1): 65–75.

Strohminger, Margot. (2015). Perceptual Knowledge of Nonactual Possibilities. *Philosophical Perspectives*, 29: 363–75.

Tahko, Tuomas. (2017). Empirically-Informed Modal Rationalism. In *Modal Epistemology after Rationalism*, edited by Bob Fischer and Felipe Leon. Cham: Springer International Publishing, 29–45.

Tahko, Tuomas. (2018). The Epistemology of Essence. In *Ontology, Modality, Mind: Themes from the Metaphysics of E. J. Lowe*, edited by Alexander Carruth, Sophie Gibb, and John Heil. Oxford: Oxford University Press, 93–110.

Tahko, Tuomas. (2022). Possibility Precedes Actuality. *Erkenntnis*, https://doi.org/10.1007/s10670-022-00518-w.

Thomasson, Amie. (2007). Modal Normativism and the Methods of Metaphysics. *Philosophical Topics*, 35(1–2): 135–60.

Thomasson, Amie. (2009). Non-Descriptivism about Modality: A Brief History and Revival. *Baltic International Yearbook of Cognition, Logic and Communication*, 4: 1–26.

Thomasson, Amie. (2013). Norms and nNecessity. *Southern Journal of Philosophy*, 51: 143–60.

Thomasson, Amie. (2015). *Ontology Made Easy*. New York: Oxford University Press.

Thomasson, Amie. (2020). *Norms and Necessity*. New York: Oxford University Press.

Thomasson, Amie. (2021). How Can We Come to Know Metaphysical Modal Truths? *Synthese*, 198(S8): S2077–2106.

Vaidya, Anand. (2008). Modal Rationalism and Modal Monism. *Erkenntnis*, 68(2): 191–212.

Vaidya, Anand, and Wallner, Michael. (2021). The Epistemology of Modality and the Problem of Modal Epistemic Friction. *Synthese*, 198(S8): S1909–35.

Vetter, Barbara. (2015). *Potentiality: From Dispositions to Modality*. Oxford: Oxford University Press.

Vetter, Barbara. (2021). Essence, Potentiality, and Modality. *Mind*, 130(519): 833–61.

Vetter, Barbara. (2023). An Agency-Based Approach to Modal Epistemology. In *Epistemology of Modality and Philosophical Methodology*, edited by Duško Prelević and Anand Vaidya. New York: Routledge, 44–69.

Wallner, Michael. (2020). The Structure of Essentialist Explanations of Necessity. *Thought: A Journal of Philosophy*, 9(1): 4–13.

Wallner, Michael, and Vaidya, Anand. (2020). Essence, Explanation, and Modality. *Philosophy*, 95: 419–45.

Wang, Jennifer. (2015). The Modal Limits of Dispositionalism. *Noûs*, 49(3): 454–69.

Wang, Jennifer. (2020). Potentiality, Modality and Time. *Philosophical Inquiries*, 8(1): 185–98.

Whittle, Bruno. (2010). There Are Brute Necessities. *Philosophical Quarterly*, 60: 149–59.

Wiggins, David. (1980). *Sameness and Substance*. Oxford: Basil Blackwell.

Wildman, Nathan. (2013). Modality, Sparsity, and Essence. *Philosophical Quarterly*, 63(253): 760–82.

Wildman, Nathan. (2021). Against the Reduction of Modality to Essence. *Synthese*, 198(S6): 1455–71.

Williamson, Timothy. (2000). The Necessary Framework of Objects. *Topoi*, 19(2): 201–8.

Williamson, Timothy. (2007). *The Philosophy of Philosophy*. Oxford: Blackwell Publishing.

Williamson, Timothy. (2010). Necessitism, Contingentism, and Plural Quantification. *Mind*, 119(475): 657–748.

Williamson, Timothy. (2013). *Modal Logic as Metaphysics*. Oxford: Oxford University Press.

Williamson, Timothy. (2016). Modal Science. *Canadian Journal of Philosophy*, 46(4–5): 453–92.

Wilsch, Tobias. (2017). Sophisticated Modal Primitivism. *Philosophical Issues*, 27(1): 428–48.

Wilson, Alastair. (2020). *The Nature of Contingency*. Oxford: Oxford University Press.

Wittgenstein, Ludwig. (1922/1933). *Tractatus Logico-Philosophicus*. translated by Charles Kay Ogden. London: Routledge.

Wright, Crispin. (1980). *Wittgenstein on the Foundations of Mathematics*. London: Duckworth.

Yagisawa, Takashi. (1988). Beyond Possible Worlds. *Philosophical Studies*, 53: 175–204.

Yagisawa, Takashi. (2009). Possible Objects. In *The Stanford Encyclopedia of Philosophy*, edited by Edward N. Zalta, http://plato.stanford.edu/archives/win2009/entries/possible-objects/.

Acknowledgements

I am indebted to two anonymous referees for this Element and my colleagues at the University of Stirling, as well as to Boris Kment, Jessica Leech, Antonella Mallozzi, Tuomas Tahko, Amie Thomasson, Anand Vaidya, Barbara Vetter, and Michael Wallner. Their helpful comments and discussion has improved my understanding as well as the Element itself.

Cambridge Elements

Metaphysics

Tuomas E. Tahko
University of Bristol
Tuomas E. Tahko is Professor of Metaphysics of Science at the University of Bristol,
UK. Tahko specializes in contemporary analytic metaphysics, with an emphasis on
methodological and epistemic issues: 'meta-metaphysics'. He also works at the interface of
metaphysics and philosophy of science: 'metaphysics of science'. Tahko is the author of
Unity of Science (Cambridge University Press, 2021, *Elements in Philosophy of Science*),
An Introduction to Metametaphysics (Cambridge University Press, 2015) and editor
of *Contemporary Aristotelian Metaphysics* (Cambridge University Press, 2012).

About the Series
This highly accessible series of Elements provides brief but comprehensive introductions to
the most central topics in metaphysics. Many of the Elements also go into considerable
depth, so the series will appeal to both students and academics. Some Elements bridge
the gaps between metaphysics, philosophy of science, and epistemology.

Cambridge Elements ☰

Metaphysics

Elements in the Series

Printed in the United States
by Baker & Taylor Publisher Services